Timothy Flint
1780-1840

THE FLINT HOMESTEAD, ALEXANDRIA, LOUISIANA
Built by Emeline Flint Thomas, *about* 1840

Timothy Flint

Pioneer, Missionary, Author, Editor
1780-1840

The story of his life among the Pioneers and Frontiersmen in the Ohio and Mississippi Valley
and in New England and the South

By

JOHN ERVIN KIRKPATRICK, PH.D., HARTFORD

CLEVELAND, OHIO
THE ARTHUR H. CLARK COMPANY
1911

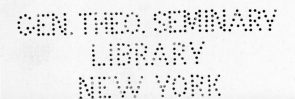

To My Wife
in acknowledgment of her help and inspiration
in the preparation of this volume

CONTENTS

ILLUSTRATIONS

He painted on his glowing page,
   The peerless valley of the West;
That shall in every coming age,
   His genius and his toil attest.

But wouldst thou, gentle pilgrim, know
   What worth, what love, endeared the man?
This the lone hearts that miss him, show
   Better than storied marble can.

— JAMES FLINT, D.D.

PREFACE

A large amount of material and that for a period for this study, where I had almost nothing else, came from Mr. Flint's grandchildren, Mrs. Emeline Flint Seip of Alexandria, Louisiana, and James Timothy Flint of Nashville, Tennessee. Family letters, photographs, newspapers and traditions—everything which could in any way aid me—have been freely and gladly put at my disposal. With them I have shared the pain in thinking of the treasures that were destroyed by the Union army in Alexandria, which burned the library of James Timothy Flint Sr. This was a very large and rare collection of books that was hardly equaled by any private collection in the south. It contained also most of Timothy Flint's collection of books and some of the manuscripts which he left at the time of his death. A more recent and unavoidable accident, the Galveston flood of 1900, destroyed a number of the books and papers of Timothy Flint which were in the possession of his grandchildren. The only portrait of Mr. Flint, which is known to have been in existence, was destroyed at that time.

I am under special obligations to the librarians of Hartford Theological Seminary, Yale University, and Harvard University for their aid in procuring books and manuscripts which could not have been obtained otherwise. The Essex Institute at Salem, the Amer-

ican Antiquarian Society of Worcester, the Boston
Public Library, and the Congregational Libraries of
Hartford, Connecticut, and Boston, I have found rich
and generous with their manuscript collections. The
librarians of Reading, North Reading, and Lunenburg, Massachusetts, the local historians in these
places, and indeed in almost every place that I have
had occasion to visit or address have been most willing
and generous in the aid they have given me in my
researches.

I desire also to express my obligations to Professor
Samuel Simpson, PH.D., of Hartford Theological
Seminary for valuable suggestions after reading my
manuscript, and to the Robert Clarke Company for
permission to use material from W. H. Venable's *Literary Beginnings in the Ohio Valley.*

JOHN E. KIRKPATRICK.

Hartford, Connecticut, May 1, 1908.

BIRTHPLACE OF TIMOTHY FLINT, NORTH READ-
ING, MASSACHUSETTS
Burned *about* 1900

The Timothy of our story was the fifth child in a family of nine. Judging by his later painful experiences in farming it would seem that he was called upon for very little work on his father's farm. He was not physically strong and was early sent to school.

From his familiarity with Salem and the sea, and from a number of references made in his later life, to Doctor Prince, of the First Church, Salem, it seems probable that Timothy spent part of his childhood and school days at Salem. He seems to have been almost as much at home there as in North Reading. Speaking, in 1828, of the First Church in Salem, he says that he had spent his boyhood days there. Speaking of the sea he says: "Many of the hours of my boyhood were nurtured in its chill and healthful waters." [8]

One of the memorable events of his boyhood, which was to have a determining influence on his later course of life, was the departure of the emigrants, from Essex and Middlesex Counties, for "Marietta on the Ohio." Among the forty-seven men who made up this company was an uncle of Timothy, Hezekiah Flint. [9] Writing thirty years later of this early experience he says of the second emigrant party that he remembered the black canvas covering of the wagon: "the white and large lettering in capitals *To Marietta on the Ohio.*" He remembered the food, which even then, the thought of such a distant expedition, furnished to his imagination. Some twenty emigrants

[8] *Western Monthly Review*, vol. i, 317, 372.

[9] Hezekiah Flint moved to Cincinnati from Marietta some time before the year of his death, 1811. His son of the same name continued to live in that city and was an honored citizen when Timothy made his home there. See also Julia P. Cutler's *Life and Times of Ephraim Cutler*, 203, note.

accompanied this wagon. The Reverend Doctor Manasseh Cutler he thinks, had the direction of this band of emigrants. He tells us that the good Doctor Cutler left an enemy behind in the person of the late learned and eccentric Doctor Bently of Salem, Massachusetts. Doctor Bently was a contributor to a local paper and took vengeance upon Doctor Cutler by writing doggerel verses about him and his enterprise. The young Timothy's imagination was not so much occupied with visions of the far away Ohio but that he learned the verses and could repeat them when he was near fifty years of age.[10]

Marvelous stories about the fertility of the new country would be told by the returning travelers at one time. Again the tide would turn and harrowing accounts of suffering, danger, and death would be told to deter the intending emigrants. All would tend to make the boy decide to see some day for himself. Concerning the stories he tells us:

> The wags of the day exercised their wit, in circulating caricatured and exaggerated editions of the stories of the first adventurers, that there were springs of brandy; flax, that bore little pieces of cloth on the stems; enormous pumpkins and melons, and the like. Accounts the most horrible were added of hoop snakes of such deadly malignity, that a sting, which they bore in their tails, when it punctured the bark of a green tree, instantly caused its leaves to become sear, and the tree to die. Stories of Indian massacres and barbarities were related in all their horrors.[11]

There are many reflections of Timothy's childhood and its surroundings in his writings. In 1828 he went he says,

[10] Flint, Timothy. *A condensed Geography and History of the Western States, of the Mississippi Valley*, vol. ii, 262, 263.

[11] —*Idem*, vol. ii, 263.

> To view once more the final resting place
> Of my forefathers, . . .

and to see the

>   . . . natal vale
> Whose trodden bounds were once my world.

It was then, resting upon his father's newly made grave that he says:

> Fond memory dwells
> On the blithe morning of my youthful years,
> When I pursu'd thee midst the new-mown hay,
> And chased the scared lark, that soar'd in song;
> Or when the darkling, wind-borne, murky cloud
> In thunder burst, clung closely to thy side.
> And now I rest me on my father's grave.
> Where has elaps'd the long, long, weary dream,
> Since, as a child, behind thy longer stride
> I gaily tripp'd? [12]

There is a description of a spring day when he was a school boy of ten. The winter had been unusually long and severe. He says:

> The vast masses of snow were beginning to melt. The birds of prey, shut up in their retreats during the bitter winter, sailed forth in the mild clear blue. The blue bird whistled; and my heart expanded with joy and delight unknown, in the same degree, before or since. The place where these thoughts, comprising my youthful anticipations, hopes and visions occurred, will never be obliterated from my mind, while memory holds her seat. [13]

"The meadows and the flower fring'd stream" of his native place were the fond delight of his memory after he had wandered far amidst nature's greater works. Of this memory and his love of nature he

---

[12] "On revisiting the Churchyard of My Native Place" in *Western Monthly Review*, vol. ii, 210, 211.

[13] Flint, Timothy. *The Art of Being Happy: From the French of Droz, 'Sur L'Art D'Etre Heureux;' in a series of letters from a Father to his Children: with Comments and Observations*, 286.

speaks in his introduction to his *Lecture upon Natural History*.[14] Still more of Mr. Flint's love for nature and of the romantic spirit of his youth is hinted at when he makes Francis Berrian explain his dreaming habits to his Mexican friends by telling them of his delight in spending hours in the rain and storm, sitting by the Atlantic in his boyhood, that when his relatives remonstrated with him for his exposure of himself and for his melancholy habits, it was in vain that he told them that such hours were the happiest of his life. While telling of this trait in his hero, the author remarks of him, that he was fully in sympathy with Rousseau, when he speaks of lying on his back in a skiff floating on a lake at the will of the winds. To gaze into the heavens under such circumstances and to give wings to his soul was the keenest delight of Francis Berrian and doubtless of Francis Berrian's creator also.[15]

The minister of a Massachusetts church, even after the Revolution, was a great man among his parishioners in almost all instances; when he served one church, as Reverend Eliab Stone did the North Reading church, for more than three score years, 1761-1822, he became a power in the lives of his parishioners that is little known in these days of the itinerant. Into Mr. Stone's parish during the school days of Timothy and his cousin James, "David Everett, a school master from Dartmouth college," came to the central school of North Reading, and "created a thirst for knowledge

---

[14] Flint, Timothy. *Lectures upon Natural History, Geology, Chemistry, the application of Steam and interesting Discoveries in the Arts*, p. viii.

[15] Flint, Timothy. *Francis Berrian, or the Mexican Patriot*, vol. i, 130, 131.

which distinguished that generation from all that preceded and that have since been born there." The influence of this teacher together with that of the minister and his son Micah, a tutor in Harvard College and later a minister, made what Dr. James Flint thought might not "unfitly be called the Augustan age of scholarship and learning in North Reading." "The result of the impulse given to the youthful mind of the place was, that five individuals of that small parish and two from the West Parish were simultaneously members, six of Harvard, and one of Dartmouth college."[16]

The school was in the building across the green from the meeting house. This building had once been the meeting house and was removed from that site in 1752 to make room for its successor. This old schoolhouse was used later for a grocery store and then for a carpenter shop. It was still standing in 1903. The meeting house of Timothy's time and that of his cousin and friend, James, was removed in 1829 for a new building, which still stands, being owned by the town and the Universalist Society[17] and used for school and lodge purposes.[18]

In the *Western Monthly Review* we have Flint's

[16] Flint, James. *Historical Address, delivered at the Bi-Centennial Celebration of the Incorporation of old Town of Reading*, May 29, 1844, 38-41.

[17] In the early part of the nineteenth century, the Universalist church succeeded to the property of the old Parish Church in North Reading. The Unitarian Churches usually fell heir to the Parish Church in most of the eastern Massachusetts parishes where there was a division between the liberal and orthodox parties. In North Reading the orthodox party organized the Union Congregational Church in 1836.

[18] See George W. Hinman's "History" in *Semi-Centennial Souvenir of North Reading, 1853-1903*.

description of the village church and minister of his youth:

> Our village had but one church, and he who occupied it, was as an angel in the golden candlestick, a man of real and deep reverence, living in the hearts and affections of the people, his goings out and comings in, noted, not for calumnious scrutiny, but from filial veneration. Those were not the days of the reign of a hundred angry and polemic sects. Religion was understood to be a matter of practise and good feeling; and the theories by which good men became religious were little investigated, the people being more concerned to gather good fruit, than to search out the elementary principles of its origin and development.

This picture has added color from the keen regret of Mr. Flint, writing in 1829 or 1830, when he said, "The same village now has its rival spires of temples dedicated in form to the Prince of Peace. . . " [19]

In one of the stories we have more of Flint's early experiences in the village church:

> I see my father at the head, and my mother and the rest of the family, according to their ages, following each other's steps through those delightful meadows, as we went up to the house of God in company. I see even now the brilliance of the meadow-pink, and I seem to hear the note of the lark, startled and soaring from our path. There is the slow and limpid stream, in which I have angled and bathed a thousand times. There was the hum of the bees on the fragrant, white balls of the meadow button-wood, which formed an impervious tangle on the verge of the stream. Each of the boys had his nosegay of pond lilies, with their brilliant white and yellow cups, their exquisite and ambrosial fragrance, and their long and twined stems. Each of the girls had her bonnet and breast decked with a shower of roses. Well, too, do I remember the venerable minister, with his huge white wig, his earnest voice, and an authority, at once patriarchal and familiar. The small and

---

[19] *Western Monthly Review*, vol. iii, 369.

rustic church was filled to overflowing with those, who had there received baptism, and who expected to repose with their fathers in the adjoining consecrated enclosure. And there, opposite to the church, was the village schoolhouse, one of those thousand nurseries of New England's greatness. Dear remembrances! How often ye visit my dreams in the desolate land of the stranger.[20]

There is no record of Timothy's name among the confirmed members of the North Reading Church. He left home for school at fifteen years of age and it is likely that his formal church relations began after that time.

The Harvard *Class Book for the Class of 1800*[21] says that Timothy fitted for college under David Everett in the North Reading Grammar School and at Phillips Academy, Andover. From the *Biographical Catalogue* of the Academy we learn that he was a student there in 1795. He entered Harvard in 1796 and graduated with his class in 1800. His old pastor, and the pastor's son also, were Harvard men, and it was a natural step for him to go to Cambridge. His most intimate friend, his cousin James Flint, was two years behind him at Harvard, though one year his senior. He mentions him later as his college friend as well as the friend of his boyhood. The class historian has an entry about Timothy that was never finished: "Chummed with ———."

In the Massachusetts Historical Society's *Proceedings*[22] it is said that he was a member of a company which gave a Greek play, at time of graduation. We

20 *Francis Berrian*, vol. i, 15, 16.
21 Manuscript in Library of Harvard University.
22 Massachusetts Historical Society *Proceedings*, first series, vol. x, 52.

know from later remarks in his own writings that he
was unusually devoted to the classics and to French.
But it is rather strange that we have no direct word
from Flint in all the mass of his writings about his
experiences at Harvard. One feels however, that
when Mr. Flint is describing Francis Berrian's impressions at Harvard there is enough of his own experience inwrought, to give us a fair understanding of
what that period of his life contributed to the future
man. He says:

> Of the character that I formed, of the impressions that I
> received at that rich and noble institution, I am not, perhaps, an
> adequate judge. . . The arrangements of that important in-
> stitution are abundantly calculated to call forth emulation, but
> I saw that emulation too often accompanied with the baseness of
> envy. I well remember, that here I first felt the "whip of
> scorpions," of disappointed ambition and mortified pride. My
> fellow students sometimes received marks of approbation which
> were denied me, and which, I had an inward conviction, be-
> longed to me, as justly as to them. My inward tortures were
> increased by making the discovery, that I was actually beginning
> to be envious. It was a most self-abasing scrutiny, that taught
> me this. I made a great effort, and I flatter myself, that I tore
> up this pernicious branch by the roots, and cast it from me for-
> ever.[23]

Mr. Flint would have been very far from saying this
last thing about himself, but to the friends of his later
years and the unbiased judgment of the historian it
seems like an unveiling of the early struggles which
produced the rarely unselfish and generous soul of the
missionary and author.

There is also a description of what must have been
Timothy Flint's early habits as a student, in the same
passage as quoted above when he describes Francis

---

[23] *Francis Berrian*, vol. i, 17.

Berrian as being in his college days, of sedentary habit, reading incessantly, and devouring everything that came in his way. The reading he calls ill arranged, judged by the better scholars. He was given to dreaming with his eyes open. Of him Mr. Flint says that he delved into the deepest mysteries of life and "investigated with a tormenting eagerness the evidences for an eventful hereafter." This last is a marked trait of the later life of Mr. Flint. Francis Berrian read also the unbelieving wits and historians; but he antidoted them with works of the immortals who have written on revealed and natural religion. From these he came to the gospel. He says: "I placed before my mind the simple grandeur of Him of Calvary." "I was deeply struck with the tender and affectionate spirit of the apostles." This converse with the gospel served to curb the ambition for greatness which was strong within him and gave to him as an ideal for life, that which should be the most quiet. Even the pillar saints of the early church appealed to him for emulation in spirit. At his graduation, Timothy Flint tells us of his hero, that he was extravagantly fond of books of voyages and of travels. He disliked the cities and delighted to imagine himself in the position of Robinson Crusoe. Again he dreamed of himself with his father's family located in the boundless prairies of the west; and again floating down from the "head-spring of the Missouri to the ocean," or about to follow "the intrepid Clark and Mackenzie over the Rocky Mountains to the Western sea." [24] All this must have been a part of Mr. Flint's own college life.

[24] *Francis Berrian*, vol. i, 17-20.

It is probable that Timothy Flint had decided to enter the ministry while in college. Dr. James Flint says, that he began the study of theology immediately after graduation. The Harvard *Class Book for the Class of 1800* informs us that he taught an academy for one year at Cohasset, and preached for a time at Marblehead. It is probable that he spent the first year after graduation in teaching, and in the study of theology. At Cohasset, Reverend Jacob Flint (Harvard, 1794), Timothy's cousin and an older brother of Dr. James Flint, was pastor from January, 1798 until October, 1835. The only item of interest which we have concerning Timothy's short time at Marblehead, was that here, July 12, 1802, he married his wife, Abigail Hubbard, daughter of Reverend Ebenezer Hubbard and a relative of Joseph Peabody.[25] Peabody was a wealthy Salem shipping merchant who was always to follow Mr. Flint with deep interest and, in the hours of the family's extreme need, with substantial aid.

Having had two years for the study of theology and some little experience in preaching, the young man was ready before he had reached his twenty-second birthday, for a settlement. This opportunity was offered to him in the parish of Lunenburg, then a part of the town of Fitchburg, and forty miles northwest of Boston.

---

[25] For items in this paragraph see *Encyclopedia Americana: Supplementary Volume*, 270, 271; Bigelow, E. V. *Narrative History of Cohasset*, 506; and Cohasset *Town Records*.

The date of Abigail Hubbard's baptism is Oct. 9, 1785.

II. THE EARLY MINISTRY IN NEW ENGLAND

As a candidate for the pastorate Mr. Flint was engaged at Lunenburg for four Sabbaths, "18th April to 9th May, 1802, inclusive." Services were to begin at half past ten o'clock in the morning and at half past one in the afternoon. Then he was engaged for one more Sabbath. After his fifth Sabbath with them a town warrant was issued, May sixteenth, in order that the town might give Mr. Flint a call. On the tenth of May the town had concurred with the church – by the selectmen probably – and was ready thus far for the formal call. But there was a long squabble about the settlement and salary. The call was "reconsidered" and renewed. During this time Mr. Flint it seems was on the field and supplying the pulpit.[26]

The call, as finally agreed upon, offered Mr. Flint "one thousand dollars for his comfortable settlement and an annual salary of four hundred dollars." The opening of his ministerial career upon so troubled a sea proved a prophecy for the future.

"On his acceptance" continues the town historian,[27]

[26] Letter of J. A. Litchfield, Lunenburg, Mass., Feb. 10, 1908, in the Boston Public Library.

[27] Cunningham, George A. *A History of the Town of Lunenburg in Massachusetts, from the Original Grant, Dec. 7, 1719 (-1875)*, 136-140. Manuscript in the Lunenburg Town Library. Mr. Cunningham died in 1875 and had not completed his work at that time.

"the town chose a committee to decorate the pulpit and secure the galleries at a cost of one hundred dollars. Another was appointed to entertain the council which was invited to meet on the sixth of October for the ordination of the young minister." We have very brief record of this notable event, but with the preparations of the town, the number of ministers and churches invited, it ought to have been, and doubtless was, a great occasion for the people of the parish and for the young candidate. The North Church of Salem, Reverend Dr. Barnard, pastor, at a meeting after church, Lord's day evening, September twenty-fifth, "declined to send their elder and delegate to the ordination council of Timothy Flint at Lunenburg," [28] but Doctor Prince and the old First Church would not treat them so. The North Reading Church voted on September twenty-sixth, to send as delegates two deacons and two lay delegates, one of the latter being the father of the candidate. [29] The old pastor, Reverend Eliab Stone, preached the sermon which was printed and sent to every family in the parish of Lunenburg. Reverend Jacob Flint of Cohasset was invited and also Reverend Mr. Bullard of Fitchburg, whose son, Judge Bullard, was to have a large place in Timothy's life in the southwest.

The town historian [30] tells us that Mr. Flint was in ill health much of the time during his twelve year pastorate, and that there was "a good deal of difficulty in collecting his salary." At the request of Mr. Flint the town voted, November 20, 1809, "that there shall

[28] Salem *North Church Records* in Essex Institute, Salem.
[29] North Reading [Mass.] *Church Records.*
[30] Cunningham, *op. cit.*

THE PARSONAGE AT LUNENBURG, MASSACHUSETTS
Slightly altered in recent years

be but one service each Lord's day." This looks as though it was a concession to the pastor's physical weakness. It was not, however, entirely gracious.

Dr. James Flint tells us that Mr. Flint carried on a little farming – the "ministerial lot" of those times gave encouragement in this direction – and cultivated a taste for letters and chemistry. This latter taste seems to have been one of several causes of trouble. Some of his more ignorant parishioners thought that the minister's devotion to his laboratory was a sign of some secret and sinful end. To this would be added their suspicions of disloyalty to the government which the "rabid" democrat felt sure was in the breast of the federalist. The charge of counterfeiting was made and it seemed so serious to the pastor that he prosecuted and obtained judgment against his persecutor.[31] This of course did not quiet the troubled waters of the parish life.

The Harvard class historian tells us of another incident, presumably in the late years of the Lunenburg pastorate, which was one of the unsettling influences. A young man of the town, who bore the reputation of a reprobate, died. Mr. Flint began his funeral service by reading one of Doctor Watts's hymns, beginning:

> My thoughts on awful subjects roll,
> Damnation, and the dead.

The audience was so shocked, and especially the relatives of the deceased, that they never forgave the minister.

Mr. Flint's plain speaking and dealing at this period of his life is quite marked. It is perhaps one of the

---

[31] Timothy Flint, in Harvard *Class Book for the Class of 1800.*

reason for his classmate's remark [32] that at this period
he was little versed in human nature or gifted in social
intercourse. A couple of stories, apropos, are preserved for us in notes in the Lunenburg Library copy
of the *Recollections of the last ten years, passed in
occasional Residence and Journeyings in the Valley of
the Mississippi*. These notes were made by Luther G.
Howard, a grandson of one of Mr. Flint's deacons,
now living in Reading, Massachusetts. He says:

> At one time Mr. Flint exchanged with the Ashby minister.
> My grandfather and Mr. Taylor went up to Ashby to hear him
> preach. He would not speak to them, being displeased at their
> leaving their own church to follow him.
>
> At another time one of Mr. Flint's neighbors called on him
> and told him what some of the people were saying about him.
> When the man left the house, the minister accompanied him to
> the gate and pointing to a place beside the fence said, "When you
> have another load to dump, leave it there and don't bring it into
> the house."

Mr. Flint was "School Committee" for three different years and for the last two years of his pastorate
he was a trustee of Lawrence Academy at Groton.
He is charged by the town historian [33] with being care-
less in his records. He made return of marriages
performed, only about once in three years and then did
not give the dates. The birth dates of his own children are not recorded and the baptisms of only two of
the three that were born to him here: Micah Peabody, baptised July 3, 1803, Emeline Hubbard, baptised June 30, 1805. Ebenezer Hubbard, according
to family records, was born January 19, 1808.

The earliest sermon that we have by Mr. Flint is

---

[32] Harvard *Class Book for the Class of 1800*.
[33] Cunningham, *op. cit.*

that preached at the ordination of his friend, Ebenezer Hubbard, Mrs. Flint's brother, to the Second Church and Society in Newbury, May 11, 1808. It is much longer than his other sermons and addresses preserved in print. It gives the impression of being too conscious of the occasion. In consequence it is formal and a little pedantic. It is lacking in the passionate and human interest that usually characterizes his expression. His theme is the motive to and the manner of the gospel ministry. He takes a wide range over the field of practical theology. There are no incidents or stories to illustrate, only passing references to the parables. There is very little of the flowing rhetoric so common in his writings. There is hardly a suggestion that looks in the direction of the heresies and controversies of the times. There is often a clear consciousness of the deeper meanings of the forms being observed and a desire that his hearers shall realize that the things which they now behold are evanescent.[34]

During this pastorate Mr. Flint published a sermon on Immortality. This was always a favorite theme. Mr. W. D. Gallagher says this sermon was written when Flint was about twenty-one years of age.[35] No copy of this sermon has been found.

The town historian, Mr. Cunningham in his *History of Lunenburg* has preserved the Covenant which was "adopted and used by Mr. Flint" in Lunenburg.

[34] Flint, Timothy. *Sermon at the Ordination of Rev. E. Hubbard.*

[35] Cincinnati *Mirror*, vol. iii, 37. In an article on Flint, Mr. Gallagher says, "The last work, we believe, which he published before the *Ten Years' Residence* was one entitled *Arguments natural, moral and religious, for the Immortality of the Soul*, written about the time of attaining to his majority."

It is given here as an indication of the undogmatic and evangelical tendency of the man:

> You believe in One Supreme Eternal God, and you devote yourself to him in an everlasting covenant.
>
> You believe in the Lord Jesus Christ, the Eternal Son of God, and you rely on him alone for Salvation.
>
> You believe in the Holy Spirit, the Sanctifier and Comforter, and the necessity of His Holy influence to your Salvation.
>
> You receive the Holy Scriptures as the rule of your Faith and Conduct, and you promise to obey the Will of God, therein made known; and to submit yourself to the government and discipline of Christ in this church so long as Providence shall continue you among us.
>
> This you covenant and promise.

Then follows the pledge of fellowship on the part of the church. There is no creed used. It would seem to indicate the position which Mr. Flint always endeavored to hold, of standing by the universal standards of the church and avoiding all sectarian creeds and forms.

There is another sermon of Mr. Flint which was preached at Leominster, Massachusetts, on the Lord's day, January 1, 1815, which shows the same practical tendency. He is not at all concerned with theology, but very much with the practical issues of every day life. He takes account of the unusual number of deaths in the parish during the previous year. There had been fifty, which numbered also their minister who had served them for fifty years.[36]

Early in the year 1814, Mr. Flint requested an increase of salary. The matter had been discussed before, and the minister felt very strongly that he was

---

[36] Flint, Timothy. *A Sermon delivered in Leominster at the Commencement of the Year, Lord's Day, Jan. 1, 1815.*

not being justly treated in this regard.   That he had a
party in the parish of like opinion is indicated by the
fact that his successor, Reverend David Damon, was
settled on a six hundred dollar salary, instead of the
four hundred paid Mr. Flint.   But there was such
hostility to Mr. Flint that when the question of increasing his salary came up in town meeting, the decision
was against him.   On the seventh of April, Mr. Flint
addressed a letter to his constituency asking for a dis-
missal and giving his reasons for doing so.   He says
he might have given many, but they would excite useless and unavailing irritation.   He wished to part in
love and in prayer for their growth in grace.   He is
compelled to give some reasons however to justify so
extreme a step on his part.   He is convinced that
under existing circumstances he can do no further
good in the parish, and this conviction has undermined
his health.   His support is not sufficient for his needs
and in consequence he is unduly tempted by his de-
pendent condition "to be timid in rebuking the evil, or
so slavish through fear of offending, as to treat the holy
and the vile alike."   From most of the people he had
during his twelve years among them, "in the morning
and prime of his life" received proofs of kindness and
affection which would endure while memory remained to him.   "Though separated here . . .
we shall soon be together again in a world where there
is no slander."   Again in closing his rather lengthy
letter he says: "While with a feeble constitution and
miserable health, I embark once more, with my family, upon a stormy world, I ask an interest in your

prayers that I may be guided into all truth and duty." [37]

A glimpse of the Lunenburg pastor's experience with late comers to church and his other trials also, are set forth in the story of *Arthur Clenning.*[38]   In *George Mason, the Young Backswoodsman; or "Don't give up the Ship,"* which is the most autobiographic of Mr. Flint's stories, there is, with a few changes of figures and names, much of the author's Lunenburg experiences put into a picture which must have been taken out of his diary rather than evolved from his imagination.   He says:

> Few of my readers would comprehend the peculiar trials of a minister in such a place, or would be able to understand the complication of minute difficulties and vexations, which, during a ministry of sixteen years, in a country village, had broken down his health and spirits, and finally induced him to ask a dismission from his people, and to move to this distant and unknown country. His parish comprehended every shade of opinion in religion and politics.   Embittered parties and eternal disputations were the consequence.   In attempting to keep clear of all, the pastor became embroiled with all.   Both himself and his wife had been reared delicately.   The salary was small, and the family increasing.   He became poor, and obnoxious both to the religious and political parties; and after sixteen years of the prime of his life spent among them, admitting, the while, that he was exemplary, of good feeling, learned and eloquent, they refused him in town meeting, a request to add something to his salary.   In disgust he asked a dismission, and it was granted.   . .   In the progress of his vexations in his parish, he had become, perhaps I ought to say, unreasonably disgusted with the condition of a minister in that country.   . .   He had been accustomed for years to allow his thoughts to expatiate in fabricating the romance of pastoral

[37] Cunningham, *op. cit.*, 136-140.
[38] Flint, Timothy. *The Life and Adventures of Arthur Clenning*, vol. ii, 146-148.

enjoyments and pursuits.   By accident the romances of Imlay and Chateaubriand, and other writers equally historical, presenting such illusive pictures of the southern and western country, had fallen into his hands.   During the long winter evenings,

> When fast came down the snow,
> And keenly o'er the wide heath the bitter blast did blow,

this romance of freedom from the vexations of a minister's life, and the miseries of political and religious altercation in a populous village, and escape from the inclement climate, to a country where he might find health, freedom, solitude, rich land, and independence, formed in his imagination.   Once formed there, all his reading and reasonings, all the opposing arguments, all the remonstrances of his friends and each renewed vexation, embellished his romance, and confirmed his purpose.   His wife, at first, argued gently against the plan; but she loved her husband, and his oft repeated, and eloquently painted views of his romance, finally presented it to her mind as a reality.[39]

Mr. Flint at Lunenburg, was beyond the zone of active theological disturbances.   The Trinitarian Party here did not separate from the old parish until 1835.   Political difficulties far more than religious disturbed him in these years.   There are some indications, however, that he was not without his troubles, and his part in the theological tempests of the time. In the dedication of his *Recollections* [40] to Dr. James Flint, he mentions as an indication of the strength of their friendship, that it has survived the "still more fatal influence of differing opinion."   Doctor Flint was an early and avowed Unitarian.   It is significant too, not only of troubles but of the peace loving man,

[39] See pages 15-16.

[40] Flint, Timothy. *Recollections of the last ten years, passed in occasional Residences and Journeyings in the Valley of the Mississippi, from Pittsburg and the Missouri, to the Gulf of Mexico, and from Florida to the Spanish frontier; in a series of Letters to the Rev. James Flint, of Salem, Massachusetts,* 1, line 9.

that in all his years at Lunenburg Mr. Flint was not
once a delegate to the Massachusetts General Association.[41] These disturbances were doubtless in the
way of a settlement in New England and a factor in
driving him to the far west where he fondly hoped
to escape from theological controversies.

Two more items are given by the Lunenburg
records as presented in the Lunenburg manuscript
history by Mr. Cunningham, and then they are silent
as to Mr. Flint and his affairs. A council was held
June 6, 1814, which dismissed the pastor. On September 3, 1815, one month before the westward journey began, Mr. and Mrs. Flint were dismissed from
the membership of the Lunenburg church to the
church in Salem. This was, of course, the First
Church, and it is probable that they remained members of this church during their wanderings in the
west and until they were settled in Cincinnati. They
do not appear to have lived in Salem. Their home
was in Lunenburg from the time Mr. Flint resigned
the pastorate there until they began the western journey – some fifteen months later.

On the twenty-fifth of November, 1814, there is a
letter of Mr. Flint written from Lunenburg to Reverend Mr. Lowell, Boston. This was most likely,
Reverend Chas. Lowell, father of James Russell
Lowell, and a classmate of Flint. He was then pastor
of the West Church, Boston. Mr. Lowell had written Flint about some family history connected with
Lunenburg and did not know that Flint had resigned

41 Massachusetts General Association. *Minutes.* See also letter of Wm.
H. Cobb, Boston, Jan. 4, 1908, in the Library of Harvard University.

the pastorate there.   Mr. Flint informs him of this fact and explains it to him by writing:

> My people were democratic, and the mania of democracy always ran high here.   It rendered the last years of my residence here very uncomfortable.   Starvation and insult exhausted my health. It has been convalescing, since I left here. I have been employed, as I observed, the past summer and autumn on a mission [for the Massachusetts Society for promoting Christian Knowledge] to the county of Rockingham in N.H.   I am now here, and unemployed.   I contemplate taking a school.   I presume you have a surfeit of applications to recommend applicants for a school.   Could I obtain a small private school, I could at least promise fidelity.   Perhaps I might add, that in former time, I had reputation, as an instructor.   If you would take the trouble to enquire, whether any such school might be had in Boston, or the vicinity, you would confer a great favor upon, dear sir, yours affectionately   T. FLINT.[42]

In the *Account of the Massachusetts Society for promoting Christian Knowledge,*[43] there are extracts from the journal of Mr. Flint, made during this mission in New Hampshire, to which he refers in his letter to Reverend Mr. Lowell: "Sept. 5, Implored God for strength, and heart to be faithful; and set out to commence missionary labors."   He spent three weeks at Kingston and six weeks at Raymond.   These places had pastorless churches, decadent from sectarian divisions and other causes.   He preached thirty-one times in the nine weeks, administered the sacrament twice, baptized two children, instructed and

---

[42] This letter which is in the Boston Public Library, manuscript department, has an interesting endorsement evidently made by Charles Lowell, as follows: "From Timothy Flint author of several works relating to the Valley of the Mississippi, etc., my class mate and friend. C. L."
"Lived afterwards in Cincinnati. C. L."

[43] See pages 53, 54, 64, first note, 66.

catechised individually two hundred and forty children, and prayed with ten sick.

It is not surprising that he did not remain with this society. Its *Account* shows a strangely sectarian view of its work as a missionary society. The "congregational church" [spelled with a small "c"] is the "regular order." Baptists of all sorts, Methodists, Universalists, "*Christyans* or Smithites" are all regarded as sectarians and their errors and ignorance are fully described. They are all regarded with the barely tolerant air of the "churchman" of all ages. Still further, this society felt concerned for the evil done by those who held to high Calvinism even though they were of the "regular order." A reading of this old missionary report would prove an excellent tonic for persons depressed by the present day denominationalism.[44]

After this date Mr. Flint held a second commission from the Massachusetts Society for promoting Christian Knowledge, and received a third commission in May, which however he did not use.[45] He is said to

[44] One of the missionary reports, and not at all peculiar, which is reported in the *Account* as evidence of the helpful character of the society's work runs as follows: "A few Calvinistic Baptists and Freewillers are of upright and unblamable character; but very few of the latter. As a body, they may be considered, as the scum of the earth the filth of creation. Lying, drunkenness, uncleanness, sabbathbreaking, fraud, and theft may be found among them, without close scrutiny; they are the prominent feature of their devotees, especially of the *Christyans* [*sic*] or Smithites. The Methodists are better in some respects; for, when they can no longer hide the abominable wickedness of their adherents, they will shut them out of their societies; and such generally attach themselves to the Smithites, and are cordially received. The Smithites, Freewillers, and Methodists, though opposed to each other, and always quarreling; yet they perfectly agree, when there is any wall to pull down (as they call it) or, in other words, a congregational church to destroy," 71.

[45] Letter of Timothy Flint to Rev. Abel Flint, secretary of the Missionary

have labored in Massachusetts.   His work under the
second commission was probably in the western part
of the state and in New York, where the society had a
mission in Essex County.   The home scene of *Arthur
Clenning* is located in New York, near Lake George,
and might indicate a visit by Mr. Flint to this section.
Another indication of the scene of his labors at this
time is a remark in the *Recollections* when speaking
of the wildness of the western Indians, and comparing
them with the eastern people of that race.   He says:
"I had, as you know, traveled in the northern parts of
the United States, and had seen the Indians of Canada
and New York." [46]

Society of Connecticut, written from Lunenburg, Jan. 23, 1815, and found in
the archives of the society, Congregational House, Hartford.
    [46] Flint, Timothy. *Recollections of the Last Ten Years*, 93.

III. THE MISSION TO THE FAR WEST

The next word, recorded concerning Timothy Flint after his New Year's sermon at Leominster, is spoken by him at the same place on the Fourth of July in the year 1815. It is an oration delivered before the Washington Benevolent Society of Lancaster and Sterling and of Leominster and Fitchburg. It was printed soon after, the Society requesting Mr. Flint to furnish a copy for the press. It is one of the important papers pertaining to Mr. Flint, because it is the only political document we have in the early period of his life and because it was spoken at a time when political passions were strong in New England. This Society before which he spoke was a political club holding to the Federal ideas. Mr. Flint himself was a Federalist, who, as we have seen, had found it uncomfortable to live in a Democratic community. But there is very little of a partisan nature in this address, and nothing of bitterness.

In his review of the Revolutionary period, the days of the Confederation, the Constitutional Convention and the administration of Washington, Mr. Flint is enthusiastic and laudatory. For the successors of Washington, he has little praise and much mild criticism. Of the French influence he is jealous. For the future of the nation he is very hopeful. Concerning New England he is eloquent, reminding us strongly of the famous eulogy of Massachusetts by Daniel Webster in his "Reply to Hayne." It is in a more tender and personal key but it has the same sustained eloquence. If it had been fortunate enough to have gotten into the school readers [47] and books of declamation, it might have become immortalized. He said:

> New England, land of my forefathers, whose habits are so congenial, whose associations are so dear to my heart, "when I forget thee," or cease to speak of thee with filial veneration, "may my right hand forget her cunning." New England – I delight to see her small but frequent farms, owned by enlightened, independent and virtuous land-holders. I delight more in the verdure and the harvests, won by laborious cultivation from native roughness and sterility, than in the indolent exuberance of nature. I love her frequent hills and dales, and the transparent beauty and the pleasant murmur of her rapid hill-streams; and would not exchange them for the creeping and marshy creeks, that wind lazily through an uninteresting and boundless plain. I admire the firm enclosures of her farms, of materials as durable and everlasting as I wish her prosperity to be. I admire her frequent and neat schoolhouses, and the courteous bow of her clean and healthy children flocking to them. And most of all, I admire her temples, the crowning ornaments of her villages; and, from the multitudes directing their steps to them on the Sabbath, I discern, that here publick sentiment still sanctifies the Sabbath of our God. And near that glorious emblem of the law, justice and order, of industry and temperance, during this life, and of a happy immortality beyond it, the village church, I survey with solemn pleasure the church-yard, seen at the same view, and associating its repose with the immortal hopes of the temple, where the virtuous "forefathers of our hamlets sleep." [48]

In this address is something of provincialism when he declaims against the party politics of the times for

---

[47] Mr. Flint's article on the effects of gambling was published in at least one edition of McGuffey's Eclectic Readers. See *New Fifth Eclectic Reader* (Cincinnati, 1866).

[48] *Oration before the Washington Benevolent Society*, July 4, 1815.

shutting out New England from the sea. This he thought, together with false pictures of "palaces, and paradises, and spontaneous wealth, in the West" was driving the hardy sons of New England beyond the mountains until, he says:

> Our dwellings, our school-houses and churches will have mouldered to ruins; our grave-yards be overrun with shrub-oaks; and but here and there a wretched hermit, true to his paternal soil, to tell the tale of other times.

The emigrants that have gone to the far west and south will feel, he thinks, that:

> They live in a state of estrangedness and exile from all that is dear to them, and dream incessantly of their native hills and valleys.[49]

There is nothing provincial, however, in Mr. Flint's outlook when he speaks of Napoleon, escaped from his island in the Mediterranean, as: "The restless disturber of the nations . . . consistent but in one thing, and that thing perpetual inconsistency."[50]

Though he is lamenting over the desolation of New England by the great western movement that was then gathering such headway; though he is pitying the expatriated sons of New England as they are spread abroad over the uninteresting and boundless plains, and dreaming incessantly of their native hills and valleys, still we are hardly surprised that he is about to join the men who, "their wives and little ones loaded into waggons, the funeral procession of New England, advanced, 'with measured step and slow,' towards the Alleghany hills."[51]

---

[49] *Oration before the Washington Benevolent Society,* 19, 20.
[50] — *Idem,* 22.
[51] — *Idem,* 19.

A letter dated Lunenburg, July 23, 1815, addressed
to Reverend Abel Flint, secretary of the Missionary
Society of Connecticut,[52] reveals the workaday life of
Mr. Flint far better than his Leominster oration. He
had been considered by the Society as a candidate for a
western mission. An offer was extended to him
through Doctor Morse.[53] Mr. Flint says in this letter:

> I have long contemplated a removal with my family to the
> westward, under an impression, that a milder climate would be
> beneficial to my health. An object, which I have had more
> especially in view, has been to establish in some central place a
> religious publication, like our religious monthly papers; except
> that it should more particularly vindicate our literature, charities
> and institutions.

He believes strongly in the importance of this enterprise, but appeals to the "better judgment" of the secretary as to its practicability. He desired the society
to give him a commission to preach in the Kentucky
and Ohio River regions until such time as he should
become acquainted and establish himself there for the
carrying out of his special plan. He says he has the
testimony of the Massachusetts Society for promoting
Christian Knowledge, that his labors have been as
great as any other of their agents, in spite of his feeble
health, and that he now holds a third commission from
that society, given to him the last May, which he has
not used. He proposes to accept the offer of the Connecticut Missionary Society, though the compensation is to be less than that of the Massachusetts Society,

---

[52] In Congregational House, Hartford, archives of the Society.

[53] This was probably Reverend Dr. Jedidiah Morse, 1761-1826, at this
time secretary of the Mass. Soc. for promoting Christian Knowledge, and one
of the founders of Andover Theological Seminary.

if he may be allowed to take his family with him and be credited with sufficient time in which to reach his field. It is interesting to note that among the references that he offers to furnish, are some from the "most respectable orthodox clergy of this region." [54]

The appointment was made for the states of Ohio and Kentucky. He was commissioned to visit such settlements in these states as he should think proper. [55]

In a letter written the fifteenth of August, also from Lunenburg, Mr. Flint accepts the appointment of the Missionary Society of Connecticut, shrinking from the idea of so much responsibility, but "having taken the best view of duty." In this letter he says further:

> I propose to commence my journey in patriarchal style, taking my wife and three children with me. May I go with the simplicity of heart, the confidence in God, and the submission to his will, of a patriarch. Should I go with such feelings, though it be to a strange and distant land, and not knowing, "whither I go," He will protect me, and make us useful, and suffer us to want nothing, that is necessary for us.

In a month's time he expected to be in Hartford on his westward journey. He did not, however, reach Hartford as early as he had planned. He spent the Sabbath, the first of October, there.

With the beginning of the trip westward, the *Recollections* commence. The missionary letters, preserved in the Congregational Library of Hartford, are also full, and the process of selection and exclusion is embarrassing. Mr. Flint sees so many people and things that are strange to us as they were to him, and he

---

[54] Letter of Timothy Flint, Leominster, July 23, 1815.

[55] *Seventeenth Annual Narrative of Missionary Service* (Hartford, 1816), 15.

writes about them so entertainingly, that one is loath to pass by much that can not be put into these pages.

The family was embarked in a two horse wagon, with such of their household effects as they were able to carry. On the fourth of October they left the "land of their fathers" and the next day crossed the Hudson at Fishkill. On Sabbath, October eighth, they were at Newton, Sussex County, New Jersey. Mr. Flint preached in the Presbyterian Church and "Had much conversation respecting the deplorable destitution of the means of religious instruction in that vicinity." Minister and missionary were agreed that there was no part of the country more in need of missionaries, Bibles, and tracts than that between Newton and the Wyoming Country, and Newburg on the Hudson and Easton on the Delaware. But this was only the first needy region that our missionary family was to discover. Every day of the long journey west, brought them new experiences of religious destitution, moral decay in consequence, of fields white for the harvest and no laborers in view. The first missionary letter[56] is full of these trying experiences, and reports constant distributions of tracts and Bibles, and ministries such as a Christian missionary delighted to give even to the stranger. In this letter there is a summary of missionary work performed on the western journey:

Arrived at this place [Cincinnati] the last of November, through many fatigues, exposures and dangers. . . I have not preached, as often as I could have wished, owing to the impossibility of doing it, while a passenger in a boat, as I have been the last ten days of my journey. On the Sabbath I have uniformly collected the boat's crew, and had divine service; and have had

---

[56] Letter of Timothy Flint, Cincinnati, Dec. 5, 1815.

the satisfaction to see them attentive, and the profanity diminishing among them. I have in a great number of instances addressed the boatmen – perhaps the most abandoned race of men in any country, that professes to be Xn. . . Since I have been here, I have been almost every day engaged in some public religious exercise. I have arranged three, or four missionary stations in large villages, in this vicinity, where I hope to labor through the winter.

Newport, Kentucky, and "White-water, 20 miles from this," are named as two of his stations.

The story of the journey westward must not be passed by without sharing the experience of the family as it is told in the *Recollections*.

Towards the latter part of the month [October, 1815] we began to ascend the Alleghany hills. In our slow mode of traveling we had had them in view several days. With their interminable blue outline, stretching hill beyond hill, and interposing to the imagination of such travelers as we were, a barrier to return almost as impassable as the grave, it may easily be imagined with what interest we contemplated them. . . Occasional samples of the people and the country beyond those hills, not at all calculated to soothe our feelings, or to throw pleasing associations over our contemplated residence beyond them, had frequently met us. The people on our route constantly designated them by the appellation of "back-woodsmen," and we heard these men uniformly calling their baggage "plunder." The wolf, the bear, and the bald eagle, were the most frequent emblems in the tavern-signs, near the acclivities of these mountains. The bald eagle itself was soaring in the blue of the atmosphere, high above the summits of the first ridge, and its shrill and savage cries were sufficiently loud to reach our ears.[57]

There were many "compagnons de voyage" from New England, "poor, active, parsimonious, inquisitive" and like themselves more fully convinced of the

[57] Flint. *Recollections*, 6.

superiority of their native region the farther they traveled away from it. He says of their experience before they began to descend the hills to the west:

> . . . It will readily be conceived that a family which had been reared in seclusion, such as ours, would be likely to drop some "natural tears," and to take a long and anxious look at the land, which contained all their ties and charities. We tried to comfort each other, as we steadily contemplated the blue summits that were just before us, that we had a world in which "to choose our place of rest, and Providence our guide." But we had already wandered far enough from home, to admit the full truth of the exclamation of Attala: "Happy they, who have not seen the smoke of the stranger's fire." [59]

This touch of homesickness is only the first of very many that they are to suffer in the coming years of their wanderings. In the first letter to the Missionary Society of Connecticut, Mr. Flint adds a note to the secretary saying that he is so burdened with the heavy traveling expenses, and with the religious conditions that he finds, that he will not continue his mission longer than six months, and then return with his family to his native state. But we hear no more of this plan after the first letter.[60]

They pressed on towards Pittsburg on one of the great lines of travel, passing hundreds of wagons. Of these wagons he says: "Many of them had broken axles and wheels, and in more than one place it was pointed out to us, that teams had plunged down the precipice and had perished." In descending the ridges many places were so narrow that two carriages could not pass. The rule in such places was that a

---

[59] Flint. *Recollections*, 7.

[60] Letter of Timothy Flint, Cincinnati, Dec. 5, 1815.

horn should be blown or a messenger be sent ahead to keep the road clear.[61]

The teamsters were an entirely new type to this New England clergyman. He says of them: "They seemed to me to be more rude, profane and selfish, than either sailors, boatmen, or hunters, to whose modes of living theirs is the most assimilated." They were for the most part drunken and little disposed to assist each other. Yet even here there were exceptions. He learned of a sort of brotherhood among them, sworn to stand by each other in the hour of need. Mr. Flint remarks that he often dropped among these profane wagonmen, as if by accident, "that impressive tract, the 'Swearer's Prayer'." Then he would note the effects as they read, some assenting thoughtfully, others merely smiling, and others again growling approval very much as Indians do at a council when they give reluctant assent to proposed terms.[62]

They met great droves of cattle and swine being driven from the Ohio country to Philadelphia, and these seemed rough and shaggy like wolves. The name of the place from which they came, "Mad River" seemed to add something to their wild appearance.[63]

While they were having all the hardships of their fellow travelers, the missionary was too much of a philosopher not to notice closely and to enjoy the human nature about him. A stage coach is broken down and the passengers sit about drenched in the rain. Their different behaviors are commented upon. A German Lutheran minister and his family are jour-

---

[61] Flint. *Recollections*, 3.   [62] — *Idem*, 8, 9.   [63] — *Idem*, 9.

neying in their direction. He is going to the "Big Miami." He had constantly in his mouth when traveling, a pipe,

> In form much like that musical instrument called a serpent, in which the smoke circulated through many circumvolutions, and finally reached his mouth through a silver mouth-piece. He rode a huge Pennsylvania horse, apparently with no consciousness of want of feeling for his wife and children, who, for the most part, trudged along beside their waggon on foot.

The plain diet of this family as they sat at table apart in the inns, consisting of "boiled potatoes, sour milk, and mush," excited the pity of the Yankee children, as their more substantial fare excited the longing looks of the young Germans.[64]

The landscape in West Pennsylvania reminded them very much of New England; but not so the "tall, hardy, lank-looking race of men," a mixture of Scotch, Irish and Germans, who spoke a "singular and rather ludicrous dialect."[65]

Arriving at Pittsburg, the new world is fully entered upon. Its vast number and variety of river craft is most striking to the eastern eye. From this point they proceeded by boat. They sold their team and wagon at a large sacrifice and found they must pay exorbitant prices for everything they bought. They were not favorably impressed in any way with this thriving and ambitious city, but they took some comfort on being assured that there was less of outbreaking evil than in earlier times.

It is not necessary to follow the family at length in this first stage of a river journey. It is to be often repeated during the next ten years and one becomes

[64] Flint. *Recollections*, 9-11.   [65] — *Idem*, 12.

gradually familiar with it.   It is needful to remember however, that the river travel, life, and influences occupied a place in the early western civilization that, in this day of railroads, can in no adequate measure be appreciated.

The hardships of the entire journey from the east were great.   Mishaps and accidents were not a few. At Pittsburg, a heavy and rapidly driven coach had collided with their lighter conveyance to the great distress of the latter but fortunately without much harm to its occupants.   The river journey was the most hazardous.   The water was low and they had to wait for a boat.   The expense of travel by steamboats, even if one had been available at this time of the year, was too heavy for the slender missionary income.   It was only four years after the time when the first steamboat had been seen upon the Ohio.   Early in November, they took passage on a crazy Kentucky flatboat, owned by a Yankee trader, and loaded with "factory cottons and cutlery."   It was a perfect day when they embarked at one o'clock in the afternoon.   The Flints were greatly enjoying the beautiful scenery, the novel experience and the agreeable change in their method of travel.   The Massachusetts trader was indulging golden dreams when suddenly the flatboat, instead of floating gently along, as its owner and passengers had expected, was whirled and tossed about in a manner altogether alarming.   The helpless craft was carried swiftly through a chute, now it stuck on a bar, and now it was dashed upon the rocks of "Dead Man's Riffle" and almost capsized.   The children shrieked, and the cotton stuffs and hardware fell from the shelves and

almost buried Mrs. Flint. The scared Yankee trader
and his reverend first mate, in their confusion, forgot
to resort to the oars, but tried to save themselves by
consulting the *Navigator*, a guide descriptive of the
Ohio and Mississippi.[66]

The reader will not wonder that by the time they
reached Beaver, the family forsook the risky flatboat,
and bought a large skiff. But the exposure in the open
boat resulted in the lung fever for Mr. Flint and sickness for the whole family. At Wheeling they were
forced to stop and take lodgings in a house filled with
other invalid travelers. Sick, neglected, in a strange
place, they helped one another as well as they could,
but were so homesick that their eyes filled with tears
at the mere mention of home. The people of these
stopping places on the river were so accustomed to
large numbers of sick and dying strangers among them
that they had become hardened and indifferent.[67]

One of the things that Mr. Flint noticed and felt
keenly was that the ministry in this section had nothing
of the kindly hospitality toward their traveling brethren, which made life so agreeable to the ministerial
traveler in New England. At Pittsburg he had been
introduced to a minister whose house impressed him
with the wealth and opulence of the owner but not
with his hospitality. The only entertainment they
found on this first journey was at the public places, at
high rates. In Pittsburg they paid double for accom-
modations as compared with Boston.[68]

After their recovery at Wheeling they embarked
in a "keel boat," one of the fastest and most graceful

---

[66] Flint. *Recollections*, 19, 20.   [67] —*Idem*, 21-26.   [68] —*Idem*, 18.

craft of the period. They reached Marietta in safety after a few days and, for the first time since leaving home, were among friends. Mr. Flint had letters to General Putnam here and writes about the pleasure of their stay at this place.

> You can imagine the rapidity of discourse, the attempt of two or three to narrate their adventures at the same time, and the many pleasant circumstances attending the renewal of long sus-pended intercourse with congenial society.[69]

Near the end of November, Flint purchased "a Kentucky flat, of forty tons burthen" and descended the river in company with several passengers besides his own family, to Cincinnati. On this last section of their journey, which occupied but a few days, they had their first intimate experience with a Kentuckian. He was a fine healthy-looking fellow with a young wife, two or three negro slaves and two children. He was a very profane man but agreed to omit his usual oaths out of respect for Mr. Flint as a minister. The wife was hopeful that Mr. Flint might cure him of his folly and make him religious like "all his rela-tives." The Kentuckian nettled the New England children by exaggerated stories about Yankees who sold "pit-coal, indigo, and wooden nutmegs." He usually followed his anecdotes by a song with the chorus:

> They will put pine-tops in their whisky,
> And then they call it gin.[70]

Stories at the expense of the Yankees they found very common. Mr. Flint thought that not even the poor Irish had so many stories invented for them and put into their mouths. He takes these stories serious-

---

[69] Flint. *Recollections*, 29, 30.   [70] — *Idem*, 34-36.

ly enough to explain that the Yankees were often made scape goats of, for people who had never been near New England. He thought also that the superior acuteness of the Yankee had made many a block-head from other sections try "to shine his hour, as a wise man," and assume "this terrific name." [71]

At Cincinnati the Flints found their cousins. Hezekiah Flint Jr., son of the man who had emigrated with the first Ohio company and whom the eight year old Timothy had followed with longing eyes, had moved to Cincinnati several years before this time. This cousin had been in the west for above twenty-five years, and his experience would be invaluable for the introduction of the missionary family to their new life and work. At Cincinnati they settled for the winter, here to get their bearings, and to determine whether to go on in the new, wild, and strange way, or to return to the land of their fathers.

The family, notwithstanding the fact that they had been raised in a small New England village, and were quiet and shrinking in the presence of strangers, seemed to have so adapted themselves in a short time to the western ways, that they soon came to be at home in their new world.

---

[71] Flint. *Recollections*, 32.

IV. ITINERATING IN THE OHIO VALLEY

The missionary family took a house and settled in Cincinnati for the winter. They found in this new city, but twenty-five years removed from the wilderness, many things to surprise them. It had eight or nine thousand people, Mr. Flint said,

> . . . Handsome streets, a number of churches, one a very large one, a very spacious building for a Lancastrian school, and other public buildings, and two commodious market-houses. On the opposite shore rose a considerable village; an arsenal of brick, some handsome mansions, and one or two country-seats, that rose still further in the distance. The buildings on each side were placed in positions, that displayed them to the best possible advantage, on gentle slopes rising gradually from the shores of the river.

Mr. Flint contrasts the free and rapid growth of this city with that of St. Petersburg which was reared by "a great and intelligent despot" who said, " 'let there be a city' and a city arose upon a Golgotha, upon piles of human bones and skulls that gave consistency to a morass." He is too true an American not to be proud of this difference and he is prophet enough to see that at no distant day the banks of the Ohio will become a continuous village, and this section in a single century become almost as populous as Europe. He was impressed with the abundance of vegetables, meats, game, and fish, and indeed, all the market supplies of an eastern city. He found provisions cheaper here, but the total expense of maintaining a family was much larger than in Massachusetts. He asserts a few years later, concerning the seven hundred thousand people of Ohio, that there are not the same number of people anywhere else on the globe so well clothed and fed as are they.[72]

He found in this city much suffering among the strangers and emigrants. He says: "It seemed to have been their impression, that if once they could arrive at the land of milk and honey, supplies would come of course." Many suffered and died and were buried by charity. He gives an incident of a family from Maine. The family was large and crowded into one room. Flint continues:

> The husband and father was dying and expired while I was there. The wife was sick in the same bed, and either from terror or exhaustion, uttered not a word during the whole scene. Three children were sick of fevers. If you add that they were in the house of a poor man and had spent their last dollar, you can fill out the picture of their misery.

Mr. Flint thought that the government ought to do something to regulate the stream of migration and that there ought to be more help from voluntary societies and from churches – the Methodists being the only body that cared for their people in such circumstances, and they did it with commendable zeal and liberality.[73]

The missionary was pleased to discover that the moral conditions of society at Cincinnati, considering its age and the materials of which it had been made, was "astonishingly regular and correct." There were many societies for diffusion of religious knowledge, instruction, and charity. The ladies had formed a

---

[72] Flint. *Recollections*, 38-40.   [73] — *Idem*, 41.

bible and charitable society. The members were highly respectable and their work showed genuine benevolence.[74]

He found the people of the city showing a laudable desire to belong to some religious society. At the time of his arrival the Methodists appeared to be in the lead. They were strongly marked with the peculiarities of their sect. They had a number of lay preachers, some of them among the wealthiest people of the town. These preachers were the leaders of partisans and sects with unhappy results. They had more esprit du corps than other sects and were disposed to use it in aid of political and other projects marked out in conclave by their leaders.[75]

Mr. Flint attended a meeting of Presbytery which was called for the settlement of disputes.[76] He says:

> The ministers took the attitude, and made the long speeches of lawyers. . . They availed themselves of the same vehement action, and pouring out a great deal of rather vapid declamation, proceeded to settle points, that seemed to me of very little importance. The whole scene presented, it may be, a sufficient modicum of talent for the bar, but manifested much want of the appropriate temper.

The press began at this time to teem with polemical religious pamphlets. He remembered the first phrase of one of them was, "It beats the devil." But he thought the religious disputes of all ages were like these of the western city, though possibly not quite so coarsely expressed.[77]

[74] Flint. *Recollections*, 47.

[75] — *Idem*, 45, 46.

[76] It is to be remembered that the New England clergymen count themselves Presbyterians when in the west at this period.

[77] Flint. *Recollections*, 46. See also 69.

One of the reasons, that made Ohio seem not inappropriately called the "Yankee state" Mr. Flint says, was that it had not only the same desire for schools, psalmody, settling ministers, and religious worship, but, "the same disposition to dogmatize, to settle, not only their own faith, but that of their neighbor, and to stand resolutely, and dispute fiercely, for the slightest shade of difference of religious opinions." [78]

It was during this winter that Mr. Flint made his first acquaintance with a new sect, called the "Cumberland Presbyterians." He could not give accurately the shades of difference which distinguished them from the older body of Presbyterians. "They describe themselves," he says, "in point of speculation, to agree with the Arminians." In the manner of their preaching, and especially as to vociferousness they copied the Methodists but outdid their model. In culture they were inferior to the Methodists, so far as he had heard them. In common with new sects they seemed to have the juvenile ardor and desire to make proselytes. He was interested in their movement to build a school where "the rough timber, which they work into the sanctuary, may be hewed with the 'axe of the prophets'." [79]

He found the ministers of the region, men of considerable talent and readiness, the latter quality being promoted by the invariable habit of extemporaneous speaking. They were also, usually men of enlightened zeal and entire sanctity of general character. He noted some peculiarities in the style of preaching in this region, which had been influenced by the pre-

---

[78] Flint. *Recollections*, 44, 45.　　　[79] — *Idem*, 75.

ponderance of Methodists and the more sensitive character of the south.   He says:

> They did not much affect discussion, but ran at once into the declamatory.   Sometimes these flights were elevated, but much oftener not well sustained.   For the speaking, the whole was, for the most part, moulded in one form.   They commenced the paragraph in a moderate tone, gradually elevating the voice with each period, and closing it with the greatest exertion, and the highest pitch of the voice.   They then affected, or it seemed like affectation, to let the voice down to the original modulation, in order to run it up to the same pitch again.[80]

Mr. Flint was pleased to think there was a growing change of taste, especially in the cities, in the matter of pulpit oratory.   Two or three well trained and eloquent young clergymen from the north, had passed through Ohio and Kentucky, had preached frequently, and had been highly popular.   These men, and the finer culture that was rapidly spreading from the schools, was working a radical change.   Mr. Flint wrote[81] to the Missionary Society of Connecticut that the character and reputation of an eastern missionary, even though he was under some suspicion as to his theological soundness, was almost too high for the advantage of the missionary when he came to preach before the expectant people.

This popularity of the New England preacher would seem to be illustrated in Mr. Flint's first winter's work, and during other periods also.   In Kentucky he often had large and enthusiastic audiences and was several times pressed to remain for a second night or until a Sunday when more people might hear

[80] Flint. *Recollections*, 47.
[81] Letter of Timothy Flint, Cincinnati, March 20, 1816.

him.[82]   He was however, often conscious of the strong
prejudice that had been much increased in this section
by the attitude of New England during the war of
1812, but everywhere he found that a man of reputable
appearance was treated with courtesy, and the "Yankee" was no exception.[83]

Among the several professions that Mr. Flint characterizes is that of the law.   In Ohio the lawyer was
generally democratic, while in the opposite state he
was a dandy.   "The language of the bar was in many
instances an amusing compound of Yankee dialect,
southern peculiarity, and Irish blarney."   "Him"
and "me" said this or that, "I done it" and similar
phrases were common, while the figures of speech
were taken from the measuring and location of land
purchases, the navigation of the rivers, and other local
interests.[84]

Whatever lack of taste and culture Mr. Flint found
in the western world, at the bar, in the pulpit and in
the press, it was not, he thought, from a lack of talent.   He found that here were the most ardent and
powerful minds, allured by speculation and adventure.
The lack of taste so much displayed in public, came
rather from the always common disposition of the in-
competent to make themselves prominent and visible.[85]

We have much in the *Recollections* about the natural scenery of the region through which Mr. Flint
traveled.   Added to his love of nature, and the keen
interest excited by novelty, there seems to have been

[82] Letter, *op. cit.*   [84] — *Idem*, 51.
[83] Flint. *Recollections*, 69, 70.   [85] — *Idem*, 49.

a purpose to learn and remember all that he could in order to use it for the printed page. There is much said about the state of society and there are many interesting comparisons made. He did not think the people of Ohio were mostly from New England but he thought the institutions of that section were very much in the ascendency, and also that Ohio was the last state toward the west where that would be true. He says: "The prevalent modes of living, of society, of instruction, of association for any public object, of thinking, and enjoying, among the middle classes, struck me, generally, to be copies of the New England pattern." Mr. Flint had not visited "New Connecticut" at this time and is speaking of the Ohio River region of the state. The more dense population, the small farms, the villages, and even the face of the country, in some ways, reminded the New Englander of his own country.[86]

One of the most interesting men that Mr. Flint met in these first months was General Harrison. He records in both the *Recollections* and the missionary letters, his impressions of and the benefactions received from this man who was then well known as the hero of an Indian war. He lived at North Bend, Ohio, seventeen miles below Cincinnati on the Ohio River. "On a fine farm," says Flint "in the midst of the woods, his house was open to all the neighbors, who entered without ceremony, and were admitted to assume a footing of entire equality." His table was "loaded with abundance and with substantial good cheer, especially with the different kinds of game."

[86] Flint. *Recollections*, 44, 45.

It was like old English hospitality. The general's personal appearance was not at first preposessing. Mr. Flint describes him as:

> A small, and rather sallow looking man. . . But he grows upon the eye and upon more intimate acquaintance. There is something imposing in the dignified simplicity of his manners. In the utter want of all show, and insignia, and trappings, there is something, which finely comports with the severe plainness of republicanism. . . There is a great deal of ardor and vivacity in his manner. He has a copious fund of that eloquence which is fitted for the camp and for gaining partisans.[87]

Mr. Flint thought that he had generally been underrated as a commander. It is interesting to note that among the amounts collected by Mr. Flint on his field, and reported to the Missionary Society, is five dollars from General Harrison, presented to Mrs. Flint, December 17, 1815.[88] But the general rendered his cause much more substantial aid than this by the opening of his house for public worship, by hospitality to the missionary when on his tours, and by hospitality to his family party when they were journeying to St. Louis. Here also Mr. Flint organized one of the two churches which were the fruit of his first winter's work, the other being at Newport, Kentucky. During this winter General Harrison urged Mr. Flint to settle in his community as the minister.[89] He had similar invitations from Dayton, Ohio, and Lexington, Kentucky.

In March, after a very severe winter, which the westerners said had been caused by the unusually large number of Yankees who had arrived the pre-

---

[87] Flint. *Recollections*, 50.
[88] Item reported in the letter of July 2, 1816, written from St. Louis.
[89] — *Idem.*

HOME OF GENERAL HARRISON, NORTH BEND, OHIO

From the original oil-painting

ceding months, Mr. Flint took a three hundred mile circuit through Indiana and Kentucky, being gone twenty-two days and preaching seventeen times, as he reports to his Society.[90]   In Indiana he was continually coming upon new cabins in the forests along the Ohio River.   He draws an interesting picture of the evolution of the cabin into the frame house, and the brick mansion; the family meanwhile aspiring to rise in the financial, social, and cultural world.[91]   There were many settlers from New England, the question of forming a state government was warm, and the slavery issue was being keenly agitated.   There was fear expressed by the southern element that it might be a Yankee state like Ohio.[92]

Vincennes, then the principal place in the state, was visited by the missionary, and also Vevay.   In the latter place he was interested in the colony of Swiss and their attempt to plant great vineyards in the forests.   He admired the colonists very much and comments on their intermarriage with the Kentuckians. He crossed into Kentucky at the mouth of the river of that name, in company with an educated young German as his traveling companion.   This German was able to see the advantages and disadvantages of the new country, and especially the opportunities it offered for the poor of his own country.[93]

In Kentucky he found the people living easily and in plenty.   The young natives seemed to him the largest people he had ever seen.   The villages were

[90] Letter of Timothy Flint, Cincinnati, March 20, 1816.
[91] Flint. *Recollections*, 53.
[92] — *Idem*, 56, 57.
[93] — *Idem*, 58, 60.

full of people who had nothing to do.   Everywhere
there were striking marks of rustic opulence.   The
public houses were full of well dressed boarders,
travelers and strangers.   The meals were served up
with much display, and the lady hostess was conducted
by some dandy to her chair at the head of the table,
which was regarded as a post of honor, and which she
filled with suitable dignity.

> I felt grieved to see so many fine young men exempted from
> labor, having no liberal studies and pursuits to fill up their time,
> and falling almost, of course, into the prevailing vices of the
> West – gambling and intemperance. . . The parents lament-
> ed the fact, and the children were ready more frankly to confess
> the charge, than to reform.[94]

Mr. Flint found the people of Kentucky more enthusiastic and national than any other western people
and looking with disdain upon the people of the
younger states.   He tells an anecdote, said to be
familiar to every westerner, about a Methodist
preacher from Kentucky preaching in a neighboring
state.   He was trying to describe heaven.   Failing in
adjectives and similies he said: "In short, my brethren to say all in one word, Heaven is a Kentuck of a
place."[95]

In consequence of this feeling and of the age and
wealth of Kentucky, Mr. Flint found that in all the
neighboring states the Kentuckians claimed and often
received a preëminence in official and social circles,
which gave them a marked influence upon the entire
western world.   He cautioned the thoughtful people
of the state against the common and acknowledged
evils that he had pointed out to them as being danger-

---

94 Flint. *Recollections*, 62.   95 — *Idem*, 63, 64.

ous not only to themselves and their descendants, but to wide regions, soon to be great and influential states. He concludes:

> Upon none of the western states is the obligation to labor for the disciplining, purifying, and, if I may so say, of redeeming the young, so solemnly imposed, as upon this.[96]

Mr. Clay had just returned from Ghent, where he had been a member of the Peace Commission, when our missionary visited Lexington. Out of consideration for the statesman's fatigue from receiving a large number of callers after his return, he did not join the procession but remarks approvingly of Mr. Clay as a statesman and a man of true culture though he may not have had the usual advantages in that direction. He regrets that so many young men pride themselves on their not having a classical education and imagining that they are following the great statesman's example. "For the one prize so obtained, there would be a thousand blanks." [97]

"Lexington is a singularly neat and pleasant town," he thinks. Not so large or flourishing as Cincinnati, but justly claiming to be the "Athens of the West," while its larger rival can only be the Corinth. Mr. Flint pays high compliment to the Transylvania University at Lexington, and to its head, Doctor Blythe who, he regrets, is bitterly opposed by the conservative religionists. The signs of general culture which he found in the homes were largely traceable, he thought, to this and similar institutions.[98]

In his missionary work during the four months of his residence in Cincinnati Mr. Flint followed the plan of "that sagacious society, the Methodists." He

---

[96] Flint. *Recollections*, 72.   [97] — *Idem*, 77.   [98] — *Idem*, 67, 68.

arranged a circuit at several points resulting, as before indicated, in two permanent churches. He was appalled by the paganism and ignorance that he found in the new and remote regions and in the river settlements, the better classes of settlers being more on the upper waters of the lateral streams.[99]

He organized several "societies for the suppression of intemperance and Sabbath breaking, the crying sins of the country." He found twenty-three families within three miles of General Harrison's place without a complete copy of the Bible, and his supply was speedily exhausted. The people had very little reading matter and had poor reading habits compared with New England people. His tracts were devoured eagerly. He had almost given offense in doling out the few he had for distribution. These, he thought, were the most effective tools the missionary could use. He says he found "the taste, the singing and the selections that prevailed here, to the last degree bad." He had prepared a collection of "slow, sweet, and solemn music" selected from European books and changed into the patent note form. He was fearful that the expense of printing, which was high there, would prevent his publishing the selections which he thought would do something to add to the attractions and solemnity of psalmody, in that section.[100]

The question of support was a most difficult and trying one to Mr. Flint. His salary from the Missionary Society of Connecticut was twenty-five dollars per month, with no allowance for expenses and with

[99] Letter of Timothy Flint, Cincinnati, Jan. 18, 1816.
[100] Letter of Feb. 12, 1816.

all receipts from the field deducted from this meager amount. In January of 1816, he wrote to the secretary that his salary very little more than covered half of his living expenses and asked that he might have his collections in addition to his salary from the society. This was apparently granted to him afterwards and was a favor shown to few others at that time. Mr. Flint found that expenses were very high in many ways and that he had little gain from the hospitality of the people among whom he preached such as an unmarried man would have had. He was soon planning to settle in a large center where he might get a more adequate support from church and school work. He found that the people in the country places had no thought of any obligation to support the gospel. He could not urge the matter without injury to his work. He was at times so much straitened that he decided to give up his mission and go into some work where he could support his family.[101] He received during his three weeks tour in Kentucky, fifty-one dollars and fifty cents in unsolicited gifts. For the four months in the Ohio Valley he reported sixty-six dollars and twenty-five cents received [102] from the field and in addition to his salary. In the later letters written this first winter, the burden had lifted a little and he apologized to the secretary of the society for the anxiety he had shown earlier.[103]

---

[101] Letter of Jan. 18, 1816.

[102] Letter of Timothy Flint, St. Louis, July 2, 1816. Flint had instructions to limit his letters to one sheet. In many cases he found that difficult and sometimes cross lines his letters. In this letter he adds an extra sheet and gives a financial report of his work up to this date. It is one of the two or three most important missionary letters.

[103] Letter of Timothy Flint, Cincinnati, March 20, 1816.

But a feeling that there was a still greater need of his work on the Mississippi where there was no organized mission work, the hope of establishing himself in a central place like St. Louis, and a letter from Mr. Stephen Hempstead * of the latter place, decided him to go on to this region. Accordingly he asked for a transfer of his commission to "the Illinois territory and the course of the Mississippi." There he hoped to be "the founder of the first branch of the Pres. church in St. Louis and the Miss. Territory." This decision was reached and arrangements made to go before he knew that the society had sent another man to that region – the Reverend Salmon Giddings. Mr. Flint thought, however, there would be room for both of them! He had been invited to settle both at Versailles and Frankfort but had declined, in part because there was an academy connected with a pastoral charge of more than one church, and he did not feel physically able for the undertakings.[104] One might be led to suspect that Mr. Flint was beginning to be infected with the same migratory spirit which he charges upon the Kentuckians, when he says of them:

* Mr. Flint had written to Stephen Hempstead on Dec. 29, 1815, as follows: "Seeing in Messrs. Mills and Smith's Journal, of their missionary tour into your country, your name given as a fit character, to whom to send bibles for distribution, I have inferred from that circumstance, that you were interested in the concerns of religion in general.

"I am a missionary from the Presbyterian church of Connecticut, sent to labor where there appears the best prospect of doing good. I am at present laboring in this vicinity, but have had thought of visiting St. Louis in the spring." He inquires also about the prospects for missionary work, the attitude of the people and the healthfulness of the climate. See *Letter* in collection of Missouri Historical Society. Copy in Harvard University Library.

[104] Letter of Timothy Flint, Cincinnati, March 20, 1816.

"Though they have good houses they might almost as well, like the Tartars, dwell in tents." He wanted to see what was in the west. Living was cheaper! Opportunities greater! The rainbow descended on the Mississippi!

V. THE JOURNEY DOWN THE MISSISSIP-
PI AND SOJOURN IN ST. LOUIS

For the journey down the Ohio and up the Mississippi, Mr. Flint purchased a keelboat about ninety
feet in length and of seventeen tons burden. At that
time there was but one steamboat which went up the
Mississippi above the Ohio and it was unsafe. Their
boat was heavily loaded, having at first several passengers besides Mr. Flint's family, and a considerable
stock of merchandise, about seven thousand dollars
worth, which belonged principally to a brother of
Mr. Flint. This merchandise was intended for the
establishment in the new country, of a business for this
brother and Micah P., the oldest son of the missionary.[105]

Many friends had been gained in Cincinnati.
Shortly before his departure, the Female Charitable
Association had invited him to preach a sermon for
them and had given him twenty dollars for his mission.[106] These and other friends accompanied the
family to their boat to see them off, after having made
many kind provisions for their comfort upon the long
journey. The breaking of ties here was a foretaste of
similar experiences that came to them many times in

---

[105] Letter of Timothy Flint, St. Charles, June 4, 1818. See also letter of
Giddings, St. Louis, March 2, 1818.

[106] — *Idem*, St. Louis, July 2, 1816.

the succeeding years and led Mr. Flint to say that he found gloomy thoughts connected with every effort to form new acquaintances, which however pleasant, are so transient and frail.[107]

The date given in the *Recollections* for the departure from Cincinnati is April twelfth, and for the arrival at St. Louis, May twenty-fourth, while the letter written to the Connecticut Society, July second, from St. Louis gives the dates as April fifteenth and May thirteenth. In view of the time that had elapsed before Mr. Flint wrote the *Recollections,* some ten years, and then far from his books and papers while on a visit in Massachusetts, and also in view of the fact that most of his journals and papers had been destroyed by a cyclone in Arkansas,[108] there need be no hesitation in accepting the dates in the letters in preference to those in the printed pages of his book, regretting only that the revised copy of this book is lost.

The first two hours of the journey down the river were most delightful, but for the threatening thunder clouds gathering in the west. The storm broke upon them so severely and suddenly that they could not make the shore and they were compelled to weather it in the open river, their heavily laden boat taking in considerable water, and all on board being thoroughly frightened. Even the grim "patron" of the boat looked serious though he had been many years on the river and many times wrecked. Because of the storm they landed at General Harrison's place the first evening and continued there a couple of days, being most hospitably entertained by him and enjoy-

---

[107] Flint. *Recollections,* 80.   [108] — *Idem,* 4.

ing the thorough work that a skilled tutor was doing with his children.[109]

Mr. Flint thinks they would have turned back after this inauspicious beginning of their voyage if they had been in the least superstitious or if they could at all have foreseen even a part of what was to befall them. It was on the second day of the trip down the river and at Lawrenceburg, that the eleven year old daughter Emeline, playing about the boat with some child of the village, fell into the river and would have been drowned but for the help of a stranger.[110]

They reached the Mississippi in ten days' time, having picked up a boat's crew of ten or a dozen men at "Shawnoe-town." This place is described as "an unpleasant looking village, that had but just emerged from an inundation, before our arriving there."[111] The boat's crew had agreed that they would neither swear nor become intoxicated while they were in the service of the minister. This agreement was so well kept, that they earned the title of "the civil boat's crew" from people on the shores and from other boatmen, who were surprised by not receiving from them the customary abuse and profanity.[112] This agreement could not, however, relieve the owner of the boat from the necessity of providing the crew with the customary "refreshments," or, as Flint says, "the usual compliment."

On the twenty-fifth of April[113] their boat drifted

[109] Flint. *Recollections*, 82.
[110] — *Idem*, 83.
[111] — *Idem*.
[112] Letter of Timothy Flint, St. Louis, July 2, 1816.
[113] — *Idem*.

into the turbid, chalk-like waters of the Mississippi and was made fast to the young willows on the shore while the crew prepared for the toilsome and perilous ascent of the river. The family was distressed by what they saw of an attempt to build a city at the junction of the two great rivers. All they found of the ambitious city of Cairo was floating on a great flat boat "a hundred feet in length, in which were families, liquor-shops, drunken men and women, and all the miserable appendages of such a place." [114]

The Mississippi opened to them a new world. It was to them as to most of the American people of that time, the "ultima Thule – a limit almost to the range of thought." The forests had seldom resounded, except with the cry of wild beasts, the echo of thunder, or the crash of undermined trees, falling into the flood. The sense of newness, combined with the sense of novelty. They "beheld everything as though the water, the plants, the trees of the Mississippi, would be different from the same things elsewhere." This led Mr. Flint to say when writing ten years later,

> Perhaps the first half day that we passed in ascending the river under every favorable omen, was the happiest period that we ever experienced, as it respects mere physical enjoyment.

In this connection he remarks:

> I have been astonished, at a subsequent passing this same portion of the river, and then too under pleasant circumstances, how much of the zest and enjoyment of such scenes are taken away with their novelty. [115]

"Under such circumstances," says Mr. Flint, "this novel and fresh scene revived those delightful images of youth, the spring-time of existence, which are most

---

[114] Flint. *Recollections*, 86.   [115] — *Idem*, 88, 90, 91.

fondly cherished and longest remembered." Charming scenery, delightful air, cheering sunshine, and the majestic view of the Father of Waters, pouring his flood between wonderful shores, filled all of the enthusiastic and poetic family with ecstasy. They seemed to float as in a delicious dream. The "huge sized cotton-woods" waved in strange loveliness. Great flocks of wild ducks and other game birds rose in airy flights from the reeds and were hardly frightened by the discharge of their guns. There were herds of deer seen now and then bounding through the distant thickets. Everything united to captivate the senses and to excite the fancy. The pungent odor of the willow flowers, which the voyagers crushed in their hands as they grasped the overhanging boughs to aid the northward motion of their boat, raised in their minds mythological ideas of "nectar and ambrosia." [116]

However, even this stage of the journey was not all pleasure. The severe and dangerous toil of working up the river, beset as it was with snags, "sawyers," wreck heaps and rocks, soon exhausted the physical energies and led to depression of spirits. They were more than once half a day struggling with all the force of crew and passengers in order to drag their heavily laden boat past a single rapid or difficult place in the river. At best they were only creeping up stream and making about twelve miles a day. [117]

The night season brought not only rest but a change of scene as well. All hands encamped on the shore. Some favorable spot was selected, camp fires built,

---

[116] Flint. *Recollections*, 88-90.   [117] — *Idem*, 92, 93.

supper cooked and couches prepared for the welcome
repose of night.   But before rest, came the social hour
of the camp.   The almost invariable rule was that the
owner of the boat must furnish for this hour the usual
rations of whiskey.   Mr. Flint probably could not
have resisted this custom even if he would have done
so.   Some of the boatmen in Mr. Flint's crew had
been hunters in the upper world of the Missouri.
Others had been "above the falls of St. Anthony" on
the Mississippi.   Some had been in Canada.   Still
others had wandered south to the Gulf of Mexico, on
the Red River and into the Spanish country.   There
were stories of river and forest, of war and hunt, of
Spaniard and Frenchman.   There were tales of dusky
loves that no feature of romance might be wanting,
Mr. Flint says, and he thought the stories would have
made tolerable romances if they had been "tricked
out in the dress of modern description." [118]

"Shawnoe Indians" prowled about the night en-
campment and were such objects of terror to the family they received little "pleasure from the spectacle."
These did not have the "tame and subdued countenance of the northern Indians" with whom Flint had
become acquainted when traveling in those regions.[119]
Desperadoes, in outlandish attire, armed with dirks,
and smelling desperately of bad liquors—"a race of
men placed on the extreme limits of order and civilization"—invaded the camp.   Not unfrequently some
lawless wretch, minus one eye, was pointed out to
Flint as a victim of the "gougers" thumb.   But the
clergyman was assured that no "gentleman" was in

---

[118] Flint. *Recollections*, 94, 95.   [119] — *Idem*, 93.

danger of being gouged. This was "a surgical oper-
ation" which they thought "only proper to be prac-
tised upon black-guards, and their equals." [120]

Two methods of locomotion were employed, in
propelling a boat up stream when poles and oars did
not answer: towing and "bush-whacking." A tow-
line or "cordelle" of great length was carried by every
boat. One of these long ropes was used after the
manner of a cable on a canal-boat, to pull the boat up
stream by the muscle of man. The "hands" would
toil along the bank tugging at the "cordelle." When
they came to the mouth of a tributary, they either
swam across, holding fast to the line, or used a yawl to
carry the rope across. When they were impeded by
a bluff, it was necessary to "warp" or cross the river
to the low ground on the other side. "Bush-whacking" was the practice of pulling the boat up by taking
hold of overhanging trees.

Crossing the river often brought no relief from their
difficulties. When the current was unusually swift
or the ground marshy on the bank, the long rope was
carried far ahead and attached to a windlass. The
boat and the boatmen were exposed to constant perils.
Mr. Flint remarks that he had never taken a trip on
the river without seeing the recent wrecks of boats,
and the red shirted bodies of drowned boatmen floating in the river. Their boat was several times in
extreme danger from the high current and from falling trees along the banks. The family often walked
on the shore when the danger was considerable. Once
while the helmsman talked with a girl on shore he

[120] Flint. *Recollections*, 98.

ran on to a snag or "sawyer," which penetrated the bow of their boat and nearly cost them their cargo if not their lives.[121]

In the first missionary letter from St. Louis,[122] Mr. Flint tells that he made most of his way on foot as the boat toiled painfully up the river, and that he could walk faster than the boat traveled. He entered the cabins of the few settlers and endeavored to learn the moral and religious condition of the people. The first settlement of any importance was the old town of Ste. Genevieve where there was some little progress and comfort. Below this he found the people without an exception destitute of the Scriptures and all religious advantages. He found little opportunity to preach during the ascent of the Mississippi but he distributed much religious literature and made known the name of missionary, which before they had never heard. At Ste. Genevieve they came for the first time upon the French mode of constructing houses and forming a village. He says:

> The greater proportion of the houses have mud walls, whitened with lime, which have much the most pleasant appearance at a distance. Their modes of building, enclosing, and managing, are very unlike those of the American. Here the French is the predominant language. Traces, too, of their regard for their worship begin to be seen. You see the Catholic church. On the ridges of the houses, or over the gates, you frequently see the wooden cross.[123]

He held an evening service at Ste. Genevieve and had a large audience principally of Catholics, in spite of their priest's opposition to Protestantism, which

[121] Flint. *Recollections*, 91, 97.
[122] July 2, 1816.
[123] Flint. *Recollections*, 100.

had recently been revealed by his order that all the New Testaments sent in by the bible societies, should be burned. Mr. Flint had such a cordial reception and invitation to settle here that he was much inclined to do so, though he decided that he would at least go on to St. Louis and confer with Mr. Giddings before he made his final location. He stopped at Herculaneum, half way to St. Louis, and had a cordial reception there also.[124]

Mr. Giddings had reached St. Louis via the northern route on the sixth of April, a few weeks before Mr. Flint's arrival.[125] The latter says in his first letter from St. Louis:

We arrived here the 13th of May. Mr. Giddings had left the ground, despairing of usefulness, and having received from the people the most pointed neglect. My reception was also cold. Mr. G. Blackburn[126] had recently been here, and had made engagements to fix himself here in the autumn. He evidently considered the mission, as standing in his way. He had made use of detraction, intrigue, and every engine, that he could move, to prejudice the mission.[127] He alternately lashed the eastern peo-

---

[124] Letter of Timothy Flint, St. Louis, July 2, 1816.

[125] Norton, Augustus T. *History of the Presbyterian Church in Illinois*, 21, 33 ff., 37, 52.

[126] Reverend Dr. Gideon Blackburn, 1772-1838, a well known and leading Presbyterian minister of Tennessee. His character is very partially and unfairly presented in this letter. Mr. Flint does him justice later in his *Recollections*, 183, 184. This letter gives us a fair picture of the not unusual estrangement between the Middle State or Western Presbyterians and the New England Presbyterians or Congregationalists as they were called later. See further on these points Norton's *History of the Presbyterian Church in Illinois*. See also Rev. Abel Flint's letter to Mr. Hempstead (Hartford, April 30, 1818), in which reference is made to Dr. Blackburn's attack on Rev. Abel Flint and New England clergymen.

[127] The mission in Missouri that was founded by the Missionary Society of Connecticut was the result in good part of the visit of Samuel J. Mills to St. Louis in the fall of 1814. See Thomas C. Richards's *Samuel J. Mills,*

ple, eastern institutions, and especially eastern missionaries, repre-
senting, that only such were sent out, as could find no employ
even in that land of dullness.   He even brought forward the
Hartford Convention.   A warning was inserted in the newspapers, intimating that our object was to disseminate the politics
of Osgood and Parish.[129]   The Americans of influence are generally Tennesseeans and Kentuckians, sufficiently disposed to cherish
prejudices against eastern people.   From this variety of concurring causes, I found almost every heart closed against us.   Our
situation, the while, was by no means enviable.   You know, that
my whole family is slender.   We had come in the boat 900 miles,
had been wet and scorched, and harassed by mosquitoes and wood
ticks, and had been suffering not a few hardships, privations and
fatigues.   No house was open to us, nor was even a hovel to
shelter us to be hired.   There seemed to be no asylum but either
the hot, leaky, and filthy boat, or the wilderness.   I dispatched a
messenger to St. Charles, 20 miles up the Missouri, but every
avenue seemed closed up there also.   On Sunday Mr. Hempsted, and Mr. Giddings, who had heard of our arrival, visited
us, and we were once more cheered with the sight of Xn friends.
I went from the boat to divine service, and we had a very full
audience, I went out to Mr. Hempsted's farm and we prayed together, and sung that fine hymn, the meeting of Xn friends, and
our communion together was sweet.   Mr. Giddings declined
preaching here any longer.   The field was unoccupied, and providence seemed to have rendered it necessary for me to fix here.

With the help of Mr. Hempstead and a young man
from Massachusetts, a Mr. Sawyer, Timothy Flint
found a two room log hut for which he had to pay

Missionary, Pathfinder, Pioneer and Promoter, 153, 154. Also letter of
Samuel J. Mills to the Missionary Society of Connecticut, St. Louis, Nov. 7,
1814; and letter of Flint to Hempstead, Cincinnati, March 11, 1816.

[129] Probably David Osgood, 1747-1822, and Elijah Parish, 1762-1825.
The former was a distinguished preacher of Massachusetts.   He was a
zealous Federalist and some of his political sermons attracted considerable
notice.   Parish was also a Massachusetts minister and greatly interested in
politics.   His election sermon in 1810 criticised the government so severely
that the legislature refused to publish it.

twelve dollars per month. They lived five days in the boat on the river. While in the harbor they had not failed to be interested in the strange craft and people from all sections of the western world.

In a few weeks' time, Mr. Flint found his audiences growing and the people softening to kindness. He felt that there was a good prospect of overcoming prejudice and establishing a religious society. He did some preaching during the summer at St. Charles and other points. He also took hold of a school which Mr. Sawyer had started and which was about to fail because of local prejudice and the timidity of the teacher. The school was conducted jointly by Mr. Flint and Mr. Sawyer. It must have been successful from the number of Catholic children who were in attendance and who remained for the religious exercises conducted by the teachers.[130] Financially the school must have been successful for Mr. Flint received one hundred and twenty dollars as his share of profits for the summer. Judged by the same standard his church work, for less than four months, was successful – one hundred and four dollars having been raised for him by subscription.[131]

Mr. Flint confessed that he was anxious to establish his school and mission so firmly that when Doctor Blackburn arrived in the fall with his teachers and preachers, he would find the ground in St. Louis fully occupied. One year later, however, Mr. Flint writes that they have united their forces and are working in harmony. He says: "We are most happily agreed

[130] Letter of Timothy Flint, St. Louis, July 2, 1816.
[131] Letter of Oct. 10, 1816.

in sentiment and in the distribution of our labors."
The third Thursday in November, 1817, they were
to form a Presbytery at St. Louis in connection with
the West Tennessee Synod. The Presbytery was
composed of the two New Englanders, Giddings and
Flint, Mr. Mathews, a Pennsylvania Presbyterian,
and Mr. Donnell, a pupil of Doctor Blackburn.[132]
Mr. Donnell was later settled over his church in the
"mine district," southwest of St. Louis.[133] The only
criticism that Mr. Flint makes on the candidate was
that he had the measles. It was most likely the first
Protestant ordination or installation service in that
part of the world.[134] If Doctor Blackburn himself had
located in St. Louis as he intended, it is not likely that
this early and happy union would have been effected.

It was only six weeks after his arrival in St. Louis
that Mr. Flint reported himself so busy with school,
pastoral duties, funerals, and preaching tours in the
country that he had little time to write and was at the
limit of his strength. He found the burden of preaching much heavier here than in the east. He says:

> Extreme caution is necessary in this abandoned country even
> in the manner of performing public duty. I should not dare
> under any circumstances to use notes. The eastern missionaries,
> who have done it have very much prejudiced their cause. The
> people here have a vast deal of effrontery, and will not pardon

---

[132] Letter of Nov. 1, 1817. See further concerning the misunderstanding
between Mr. Flint and Doctor Blackburn in the letter of the former to Mr.
Hempstead from St. Charles, Nov., 1816.

[133] — *Idem*, St. Charles, May 4, 1818. Flint says of this district: "I
saw in the excursion and in the many families, that I entered in the mine
district far more encouraging appearances, than I have noted elsewhere in
this country. There are many respectable and serious families from Connecticut. You will fancy, that we were most cordially received."

[134] Flint. *Recollections*, 127.

modesty in anyone. A frothy and turgid kind of ready eloquence is characteristic of every class of public speaker. I have broken over all early habits, and have triumphed over extreme reluctance, and against my own taste and feelings, have become all things to all people, as far, as I possibly could. They think, that were I not extremely feeble, I should be almost, except my eastern bonds, as a Kentuckian.[135]

Contrary to his hopes he found living expenses here higher than in Cincinnati and was still perplexed by this matter. He was encouraged, however, when he looked back over the long and expensive way that he had come, for it seems almost as if the ravens had provided.[136]

The business of his brother, in which Mr. Flint had invested about one thousand dollars, did not he says occupy any of his time. He was not usually in the store more than once a week. It proved not only an unsuccessful business but the occasion of much criticism later. It was, very possibly, an occasion of hostility to his ministry at this time.[137]

During the first summer Mr. Flint distributed one hundred and fifty Bibles, part of them French. He observed that he often found during his travels large deposits of Bibles in the hands of public men, who had agreed to act as officers of the societies formed by Mr. Mills, lying unused, while there were many families all about without a copy of the Sacred Book. He thought political men poor agents for such work.[138]

Toward the close of his work in St. Louis he held a communion service, the first Protestant service of the

---

[135] Letter of Timothy Flint, St. Louis, July 2, 1816.
[136] — *Idem.*
[137] Letter written from St. Charles, June 4, 1818.
[138] Letter from St. Louis, July 2, 1816.

kind there. The people were from all states and
sects and each one thought that his way of conducting
the ceremony ought to be adopted and was scandalized
that so much concession should be made to others.
Mr. Flint thought when writing nine years later [139]
that this occasion had brought out in an unusual way
people's attachment to form. It was, however, a very
solemn and affecting service and he thought marked
the beginning of a religious profession for some of the
younger people. [140]

In this connection, Mr. Flint's remarks about the
sects beyond the Mississippi are interesting to notice.
He says:

> At one point you meet with a respectable Methodist, and
> begin to feel an attachment for the profession. He next meets
> you with harmony and coöperation on his lips, and the next thing
> you hear, is, that you are charged with being a fierce Calvinist,
> and that you preached that "hell is paved with infants' skulls."
> While, perhaps the society, with which you are connected, hear
> from an opposite quarter and from a pretended friend, that in
> such a sermon you departed from the dicta of the great master,
> and are leading the people to the gulph [sic] of Arminianism.
> The Baptists are as exclusive as in the older regions. Even
> among our own brethren [It is always to be remembered that
> the New England missionaries at this time are Presbyterians as
> soon as they cross the Alleghany mountains, and by a process
> much simpler and less difficult than such crossing.], it is well
> known, that there is some feeling of a questionable nature, some
> rivalry between the pupils, the doctors, and schools, of Andover
> and Princeton.

He mentions besides the usual sects the followers of
Elias Smith and speaks of numerous other would-be-
founders of sects. The people in general are fully

---

[139] Flint. *Recollections*, 112.
[140] Letter of Timothy Flint, St. Charles, Oct. 10, 1816.

persuaded that they have done their full duty toward a preacher when they have listened to what he has to say.[141]

The western missionary's life, he thinks, is as hard and dangerous as the foreign. He laments, that when the former falls, as he so often does, he is unrecorded, though he "who falls in a foreign land, is lamented as a hero and a martyr. Provision is made for his family, and the enthusiasm and regret of romantic sensibility attach to his memory."[142]

Mr. Flint removed to St. Charles early in September. He found that he could not continue his school and his missionary work, and he preferred to give up the former. St. Charles was a much more central location for the circuit of preaching points which he visited, especially up the Missouri River. He thought that at this point where the great rivers were but four miles apart would be the center of population rather than at St. Louis. It was then the political center of the territory. He also mentions as one of the reasons for his leaving St. Louis that the people there, while they attended his service in good numbers and from the country regions round about were for the most part young men and women on whom all instruction and exhortation seemed wasted. There was, too, "the Catholic mummery," the ridiculousness of which was only exceeded by the heedlessness with which it was witnessed by the Catholics themselves. Duels were continually occurring and all was confusion and uproar. It seemed as though even the sentiment of a God was universally erased, and the wick-

[141] Flint. *Recollections*, 114, 115.   [142] — *Idem*, 115.

edness of the place threw a continual gloom over his mind which he felt he was not able to bear. He had not lived in St. Charles and it at least looked better in these respects besides having the advantages above named.[143]

In later days and in more philosophic moments Mr. Flint speaks more favorably of the Roman Catholics, of sectarianism, and even of the moral conditions of this new country. But what is recorded in this chapter is out of the immediate and bitter experience of the man in the midst of conditions which in a moral and social way is described by other missionaries and travelers in not very different terms.[144]

Mr. Giddings took up the work of the school and pulpit in St. Louis upon Mr. Flint's departure, and thought he saw signs of improvement above what he had first found. He was sufficiently encouraged to try to carry on the work unless Doctor Blackburn should undertake it or make it impracticable for him to continue. At any rate Mr. Giddings [145] was the mis-

[143] Letter of Timothy Flint, St. Charles, Oct. 10, 1816.

[144] See especially Rufus Babcock's *Memoirs of John Mason Peck* (Philadelphia, 1864), 85-88.

[145] Letter of Salmon Giddings to the Missionary Society of Connecticut, St. Louis, Sept. 20, 1818.

Mr. Giddings in this letter gives an interesting report of the Presbyterian churches in Missouri territory.

	When Formed	No. of Members When Formed	No. Re-moved	No. Re-ceived	Present No.	Baptized	
						Adults	Infants
Concord Ch., Belleview	Aug. 3, 1816	27	8	21	40	1	12
Bonhome	Oct. 18, 1816	16	5	4	15	2	6
St. Louis	Nov. 15, 1817	10		5	15	1	2
Union Church of Richmond & Dry Creek	Apl. 17, 1818	7			7		
Church of Buffaloe	May, 1818	14			14		
Church of St. Charles	Aug. 29, 1818	9			9		

sionary there for a number of years, and organized the First Presbyterian Church, November 15, 1817. In all accounts the writer has seen, Giddings is spoken of as the first resident pastor in St. Louis. With how much justice this claim is made can only be judged when we consider Mr. Flint's reports to the Missionary Society of Connecticut. Unfortunately, Mr. Giddings's reports for 1816 and 1817 are missing from the files of the society.

VI.   ST. CHARLES AND SURROUNDING REGIONS

Mr. Flint made his home in or near St. Charles, Missouri, for four years.   Three of these years, 1816-1819, were spent in missionary and ministerial work. The last year, 1821-1822, was spent on a farm near St. Charles.   At present the missionary period only is of interest.

For this time we have a greater abundance of material than for any other of his life, except possibly, the Cincinnati years, 1827-1833.   One hundred pages of the *Recollections* are devoted to his work, experience, and observations here; there are six letters written to the Missionary Society by Mr. Flint from St. Charles, and three letters written to the same society at this time by Reverend Salmon Giddings, which largely concern Mr. Flint.

This period is important in the life of the eastern minister and his family for it marks the notable and painful process of physical and social acclimatization, which all had to undergo; a process which often meant death on one hand and moral disaster on the other, to a fearfully large per cent of the western home seekers. A few months after his arrival we notice Mr. Flint flattering himself that he had so far adapted himself to the western ways, as to be almost "like a Kentuck-

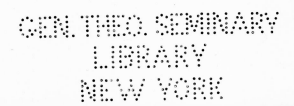

ian." In this he finds himself later painfully disappointed.

This period is important again because of Mr. Flint's fully recorded experiences in the new and formative society of which he was a part. It is full of significance for the historian and the student of society. We can do no more than mention some of the things that seem most significant from this point of view, since they are not vital to the life story of Timothy Flint.

Mr. Flint traveled constantly and widely in his missionary work at this time, going frequently along the main lines of travel, fifty and one hundred miles from his home. He was always keenly alive to all that was to be seen and heard. These experiences were not lost or greatly changed by time. It has been of much interest to the writer to compare the reports made to the Missionary Society of Connecticut and the impressions of the same conditions as they are recorded in the *Recollections* and written several years later and under very different circumstances. There is a difference of course but it is easily accounted for and it does not argue against the accuracy and finality of Mr. Flint's judgment upon men and affairs.

Of those things of general interest in the experiences and records of Mr. Flint for this period, the most noticeable is the emigration of the times. At St. Charles in the fall of 1817, there was an average of one hundred people every day coming to the town, or passing to near-by points. Nearly all were poor and not one family in fifty had a Bible.[146] He remarks on

---

[146] Letter of Timothy Flint, St. Charles, Nov. 1, 1817.

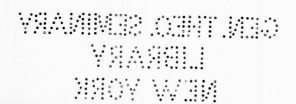

the fads which seized the moving streams of people
to go to a certain point for a few months, as the Boon's
Lick, on the Missouri, only to branch off in a few
months to Salt River.[147] He speaks of the instability
of the population – no one felt settled enough to build
a good house, plant an orchard, or aid in building
church or school.[148] He is concerned with the effect
of the new comers on the old and settled French society.   There, all the vices had indeed found lodging,
but the people were quiet and inoffensive in their sins.
But with the flood of newcomers all gates were swept
away.   A movement, that was well under way for the
erection of a meeting house in St. Charles and for se-
curing a churchyard, was dissipated by the inrush of
strangers.   The revelry of the dance and drinking
places continued on the Sabbath day until the minister
reported the condition to the grand jury.   The jury
acted and checked the disgrace.   But the revelers –
and only a few heads of families did not have a part in
it – were so offended with the disturber of their pleas-
ures that they soon found means of displacing him.[149]

The different classes of frontiersmen, emigrants,
and village people are noted and commented upon at
length.   Mr. Flint had a wide experience with the
Indians in these years, both by visiting them in their
villages, and in seeing great councils gather at St.
Charles for conference with the government agents,
and for trading purposes.   They came from the west
as far as the Rocky Mountains.   He was greatly interested in these native peoples and made a close study

[147]   Flint. *Recollections*, 203, 204.
[148] — *Idem*, 204, 206.
[149] Letters of Timothy Flint, St. Charles, Aug. 3, 1817, and June 4, 1818.

of them.[150] The intermarriage of the French and Indians, with its results, is commented upon.[151]

The methods of laying out, advertising, and selling real estate, farms, and town sites is noticed.[152] This description seems quite modern to residents of the recent west and to the present day investors of the older states who have been tempted to buy western property. He discusses the American habit of "puffing" and especially its western development as it affects the newspapers, schools, and general culture.[153] The crudity and the cruelty of society is commented upon, causing on the one hand, an entire disregard of literature among people who are so busy with merely physical things; and on the other hand, as shown in the constant dueling and frequent murders.[154] These conditions together with rowdyism and the violation of the Sabbath, Mr. Flint thought, were quite visibly and immediately affected by the gathering of the best elements into a religious society, under the leadership of competent ministers. He wished that eastern people, who talk about the felicity of a country without institutions of religion, might have an opportunity such as he had to experience that imagined felicity.[155]

Mr. Flint at this time, and in all his writings upon the west, brings to mind a fact largely forgotten about the westward movement of populations, namely, the

---

[150] See his *Recollections*, 135-164. Also the *Indian Wars*, the *Geography and History, Daniel Boon* and the *Shoshonee Valley*.

[151] Flint. *Recollections*, 131, 163.

[152] — *Idem*, 130.

[153] — *Idem*, 185-188.

[154] — *Idem*, 178-183.

[155] Letter of Timothy Flint, St. Charles, Nov. 1, 1817

enormous cost in human suffering and life. His description of the "seasoning" fevers which invariably overtook the emigrant of whatever age or physical condition, brings to realization the price that was paid in making the west to blossom and to build up its civilization. Mr. Flint shows his subtle power of analysis and portraiture in describing the highly wrought mental states, conditioned by fever and delirium. For two months, August and September, 1818, he was himself in the supposedly fatal grip of the seasoning fever. It was one of those states of delirium when the mind is abnormally acute. He could repeat verses which were impossible for him under normal conditions. All the foreign languages he had studied he could use with surprising facility. All care and concern for life had passed and he felt as though in a dream world. The first symptoms of returning strength and recall to earth were distressing. The spiritual exhileration and renewal which remained with him during and after convalescence, show the fine religious and moral balance of his character and in a measure account for the noble mastery of the very trying episode noticed in the closing paragraphs of this chapter.[156]

Still one other thing of general interest is more closely related to this period of his western experience than to any other – the mounds and other relics of the prehistoric American races. In many directions of his travels he noted these curious ancient formations, speculated on their age and uses, and took advantage of every opportunity to examine the contents of the mounds, ancient settlements and cemeteries. Near

[156] Flint. *Recollections*, 132-135.

St. Charles he believed there had once been a very
dense population as he believed there would be again.
While on a journey up the Illinois River he was interested in the mounds in the Cahokia prairie.   His son
Micah probably accompanied his father at this time
for he wrote a poem on these mounds, dated March
19, 1825, which Mr. Flint included in the *Recollections*.[157]   Just back of the house on his farm below
St. Charles at Point Prairie or the Mamelle there
were two of these artificial mounds.   While digging
a ditch in this vicinity, the Flints discovered some interesting relics which he describes, together with relics
found near St. Louis at the time of his residence
there.[158]

Mr. Flint was always interested in the bar and gives
us his impressions of several leading lawyers of the
territory.[159]   There were two sessions of the legislature
at St. Charles during his residence there.   He says
of the legislators:

> Some of them were neither Solons nor Solomons.   Indeed, in
> the western country and elsewhere in America, they do not believe
> in the maxim, "ex quolibet," etc.; almost any timber can be
> worked into the political ship.   Some boys invented a very toler-
> able pasquinade.   It was labelled on the plastering around the
> speaker's chair. "Missouri, forgive them.   They know not what
> they do." . .   I was here [i.e. in the state.   He was in Jack-
> son in 1821 when Missouri became a state] when the state of
> Missouri passed from its territorial character to that of a state.
> The slave question was discussed with a great deal of asperity,
> and no person from the northern states, unless his sentiments

157 Flint. *Recollections*, 167-169.

158 Flint. *History and Geography of the Mississippi Valley*, vol. i, 126-
129; *Recollections*, 164-174.

159 Flint. *Recollections*, 184, 185.

were unequivocally expressed, had any hope of being elected to the convention, that formed the constitution. The constitution was well enough, except in its stupid interdiction of ministers from being eligible to any office in the state, and in some other trifling enactions equally barbarous.[160]

Of preachers as he met them at this time, he says: "Of the itinerant preachers, I did not hear one who approached to mediocrity. They may have been pious men, but, for the most part, they defy all criticism." He several times speaks of a minister in St. Louis, who was for a time popular as an orator, and who made great pretense of learning and as a teacher. He does not name him but it was probably John Mason Peck that was in mind. Mr. Flint's estimate of this pioneer,[161] if it be he, is not as high as the present generation would rate him, judging him by his life work.

The Reverend Dr. Blackburn, who figured so considerably in the anticipations of Mr. Flint and his companion, Mr. Giddings, is spoken of, as one of the western type of preachers. He says:

I heard the Rev. Dr. B. the favorite orator of Tennessee, preach. I would not wish to laud him in the same affected strain, with the encomiums of the blind minister of Virginia. But he is certainly an extraordinary man in his way. His first appearance is against him, indicating a rough and uncouth man. He uses many low words, and images and illustrations in bad taste. But perhaps, when you are getting tired, almost disgusted, everything is reversed in a moment. He flashes upon you. You catch his eye and you follow him; he bursts upon you in a glow of feeling

---

[160] Flint. *Recollections*, 214, 215.

[161] — *Idem*, 183.

Mr. Peck speaks more plainly and even less justly of Mr. Flint. He says that his sermons while good and sometimes eloquent were borrowed from published sources such as Burder's *Village Sermons*. See Houck's *History of Missouri*, vol. iii, 229, 230.

and pathos, leaving you not sufficiently cool to criticise. We may affect to decry the talent of moving the inmost affections. After all, I am inclined to think it the most important qualification, which a minister can possess. He possesses this in an eminent degree. He has the electric eye, the thrilling tones, the unction, the feeling, the universal language of passion and nature, which is equally understood and felt by all people. He has evidently been richly endowed by nature; but his endowments owe little to discipline or education.[162]

Rather a generous criticism, is it not, of a man who had warned the people as Doctor Blackburn had done in St. Louis, against "the New England emissaries of the Hartford Convention."

He adds a word about the New England preachers: there are a few of them, "plain men, of sound instruction and good sense, who are respected for these qualifications, but are not popular as orators."[163]

We must turn now to things more intimately connected with Mr. Flint. Among the earliest difficulties in the new work at St. Charles was that of finding a place to live. Rent, Mr. Giddings says, cost the Flint family twelve to twenty dollars per month. His total income from his professional labors for the two full years of service here was considerably under four hundred dollars annually. During his first year in the territory, he lived in six different houses. Then he was driven out of a comfortable cottage, by a "powerful Kentuckian with a host of negroes," into a thirteen by fourteen foot log hut with a ground floor, and Mrs. Flint's school for young ladies was broken up. It was at this time that the family set about to secure a house of their own, as a measure of economy and neces-

---

[162] Flint. *Recollections*, 183, 184.
[163] — *Idem*, 184.

sity, after having moved four times in a year.[164] Upon
this house the minister labored with his own hands
during the week, to the scandal of some of his southern
neighbors.[165]   In the new cottage the school was resumed.   Some of their most pleasant experiences
and friendships came through their schools.[166]

Bible and tract distribution continued to be an important part of his work.   He apparently thought it
even more effective than preaching.   He gives some
incidents of its effectiveness.   He had as high as twenty calls in one day for Bibles.   He thought five hundred would not satisfy the demands.[167]   Mr. Giddings
had a similar experience.   Mr. Flint had at this time
published his collection of hymns.   He was teaching
the people to sing them, being usually his own chor-
ister as all western ministers were at that time.   He
occasionally opened a preaching point at some new
place, nearby or as far as forty miles up the Missouri,
and again thirty miles up the Mississippi, at Cuivre.
At this latter point seven persons wished to form a
church society and a like number at St. Charles wished
to take the same step.   Mr. Flint discouraged this
move, thinking the numbers too small and their indi-
vidual character unfit for so important an undertaking.   He did urge however, the building of churches
or meeting houses.[168]   This cautious disposition is one
of the charges later against Mr. Flint – as showing in-
competency.   He reports audiences at all points as

[164] Letter of Timothy Flint, St. Charles, Nov. 1, 1817.
[165] Letter of Jan. 4, 1818.
[166] Flint. *Recollections*, 194-197.
[167] Letter of Timothy Flint, St. Charles, April 15, 1817.
[168] *Idem.*   Also letters of Aug. 3, 1817 and June 4, 1818.

growing during the first year, and it would seem that he was always regarded in this section as an eloquent and able preacher. Mr. Giddings so regarded him. In the second year Flint says, that to speak accurately he must say that his audiences are not growing, except at Bonhome, where a church was organized October 18, 1816.[169] He was compelled to say also that moral conditions were no better. He felt that there had been too much coloring of missionary reports in order to suit the eastern constituency of the society. There were occasional cases of seriousness which he reported from time to time but the burden of sin seemed to bear down with crushing force at this period.

During part of his St. Charles labors he turned pedestrian, both from motives of economy and health. He walked eighty miles in one week, and in seven weeks crossed the Missouri sixteen times. One year he did not receive more than enough money south of the river to pay his ferriage. It was always dangerous and many people lost their lives in crossing this river, yet he came to love the muddy stream so much that when he returned to it after an absence of two years he wrote some of his most interesting lines upon it.[170]

He was continually occupied from dawn until ten at night. His frail wife was not less driven with her school and home duties. Many of his business letters, and letters to his friends were written on a plank in some cabin during his journeys in the country.[171] He

---

169 Letter of Salmon Giddings, Sept. 20, 1818; also of Timothy Flint, May 4, 1818.

170 Flint. *Recollections*, 289-291.

171 Letter of Timothy Flint, April 15, 1817.

had often been lost on the prairies, and again he had been charmed with the glory of the prairie fires, as seen in the distance at night.

In spite of his philosophy, breadth, and geniality, the evils about him, and the burdens upon him, together with his natural disposition for plain speech, and his New England notion of the ministry, led the missionary to such pointed condemnation of the open sins of his village and to take such steps against them, that during the second year of his residence, he had almost the entire community hostile to him. Even his friends at other places and his fellow ministers joined in the condemnation.[172] He says he did not then speak French well enough to preach in it but that he could and did use it to reprove and warn. He declares that Hindustan can not be more heathen than is their village, and it is not worse than others. In his letter of April 15, 1817, he gives the following picture of moral conditions:

The sinners are most of them the worst of all — Gospel sinners — who have relinquished, and lost all, that they once had, or knew, or heard in a more favored country. The sick have no guidance — the dying no voice of prayer. The dead are carried unhonored, and almost unmourned to their long home. There is not to my knowledge a consecrated American burial ground in the whole territory. I tremble for the influence of the general example upon my family and myself; and I am here feeble, and alone to contend for the cause of the blessed Redeemer. When my own heart is discouraged and cold, and these periods return too often, I am ready to imagine, that there is in the very atmosphere, which we respire here, a moral miasma fatal to religious sensibility. As for natural sensibility, I am sure there is little here. The people have all broken the tenderest ties in coming

172 Letters of S. Giddings, St. Louis, Jan. 5, March 21, and May 23, 1818.

here.   They have all witnessed great trials, and difficulties in
passing these wide wildernesses.   They have witnessed the dreadful atrocities of the savages.   They have to struggle with the
obstacles peculiar to a new country, and scenes of suffering, which
make the hardest eastern heart thrill, produce here no impression.

A man who could feel and write in this strain would
be sure to do some preaching, which would go close
home.   So strongly does he feel that he is doing no
good that he writes in August of this year that he
must soon cease to take any money from the society.
He thinks it is consecrated money and should not be
wasted where it is in no way appreciated.   It was
at this time that he attacked the Sunday balls.   The
first day he preached here, there had been a horse race
which started off just as he rode up to the preaching
place, and but a few yards away.[173]   But the Sunday
balls as a new and regular thing were more than he
could stand.   He wrote to the secretary of the Missionary Society of Connecticut that he had threatened
to report the offenders to the grand jury.   Later he
did so and they were punished by authority of the
law.   This extreme measure together with some other
grievances against Mr. Flint brought his labors to a
close.

The whole story is told in three of Mr. Giddings's
letters to the Missionary Society of Connecticut.[174]
It is a painful story, even as read in these almost century old letters.   They are ungenerous letters, reflect-
ing on the judgment of a good man, gone more
than three quarters of a century to his reward.   Had

---

[173] Flint.   *Recollections*, 125.

[174] See note 172.   See also letter of Rev. Abel Flint (Hartford, April
30, 1818), to Mr. Hempstead.   The latter had reported some of Mr. Flint's
difficulties to the Missionary Society of Connecticut.

it not been for his full reporting of the matter to the
Missionary Society, we should have been in ignorance
of any special difficulties in Mr. Flint's life at this
time, or of the part which Mr. Giddings had in the
matter, a part which clearly led to Flint's resignation
of his mission. This result was not expected nor desired by Mr. Giddings.[175] Although he was younger
than Mr. Flint, had thirteen or fourteen years less
experience in the ministry, and had gone west later
than Mr. Flint, Mr. Giddings constituted himself,
apparently, the head of the mission. In this capacity,
it appears that he had reported to Reverend Abel
Flint, secretary of the Missionary Society of Connecticut, late in 1817, that there were damaging rumors
afloat concerning Mr. Flint. The secretary asked for
particulars. Mr. Giddings had not expected to have
his remarks about his neighbor taken so seriously and
he was reluctant about going into details. However,
this request led Giddings to report, January 5, 1818,
that the rumors had grown and that the people were
universally prejudiced against Mr. Flint. For reasons which Giddings names but which charity
forbids us to mention he did not at this time make a
detailed statement. In March, however,[176] he made

[175] Salmon Giddings, 1782-1828, was a native of Hartford, Conn., graduated at Williams College, 1811, and at Andover Theological Seminary, 1814.
He was tutor for one year at Williams after his theological course and then
went to St. Louis under the Missionary Society of Connecticut, arriving a
few weeks before the Flint family. He seems to have been a plain, honest,
plodding man of ordinary abilities, not physically strong but faithful and
largely efficient in the new world where his few years of work were accomplished. On Giddings's life and work see Augustus T. Norton's *History
of the Presbyterian Church in the State of Illinois*, 21, 33 ff., 37, 52. J. E.
Roy's "Salmon Giddings" in *New Englander* (New Haven, 1874), vol.
xxxiii, 513-532.

[176] Letter of S. Giddings, St. Louis, March 21, 1818.

a particular statement. The charges against Mr.
Flint summed up by the writer after he had investigated them are: "He is a Speculator, Avaricious,
Immoral and of course, not a Christian." Mr. Giddings says further in this letter that he has investigated
many of the worst reports, traced them to their origin,
"and found them to be the offspring of malice and
without foundation, or at least very little to make any
of them from."

Two months later[177] Mr. Giddings reports that
there is not nearly so much talk, feeling has subsided
and that the better class of people have restored Mr.
Flint in their good opinion. He thinks that the talk
will blow over entirely and he hopes that Mr. Flint
may be retained in the mission. He is very uncomfortable over his part in the affair and adds a closely
written note, and a cross line postscript to explain
himself. But it was too late to recall what he had
said and done. It seems to have been the mistake of
an honest but overofficious and inexperienced man,
zealous for the success of the common work.

The grounds for all the charges had been, Mr.
Flint's plain speaking, his rebuking of outbreaking
sins, his connection with a business enterprise at St.
Louis, his endeavors to extricate himself from the debt
that had resulted from his business failure and his
family expenses, and especially his purchase and location of a land claim on an island above the town, where
the people had long been accustomed to get their
wood supply at the expense of the government. Here,
when he forbade the removal of timber, Mr. Flint ran
squarely against the age long and instinctive belief of

[177] Letter of May 23, 1818.

European peoples that public lands are Commons and that any public or private interference with these rights should be resented vigorously. He speedily disposed of this claim and re-located[178] below the town at Point Prairie.

Mr. Flint did not know until the third of June that his difficulties had been reported to the Society. He probably heard of it from Mr. Giddings while he was at St. Louis where he had regular preaching appointments, on days when Mr. Giddings was absent. Mr. Flint does not connect his fellow missioner with the reports, but lays the responsibility on a Mr. Beebe who had lately been in Hartford. The letter* in which Mr. Flint resigns his mission and reviews his work with the society, and in which he refers briefly to the charges made against him, is in many ways the best now extant.

Judged by this letter and by his remarks in his *Recollections* several years later, Mr. Flint did not give Mr. Giddings the slightest occasion to confirm his notion that he was a man of quick or uncontrolled temper.[179] Mr. Flint declared that he had loved Mr. Giddings, that he had put his pride under and yielded to his judgment in matters pertaining to the mission and that he had taken the place assigned to him – that of a subordinate. Mr. Giddings letters also show that this was the relationship between them. Mr. Flint makes no elaborate attempt to defend or explain himself and takes a dignified and grateful leave of the Missionary Society.[180]

[178] Mr. Gidding's letter of March 21, 1818.
* See Appendix B.
[179] Letter of Jan. 5, 1818.
[180] Letter of Timothy Flint, June 4, 1818.

VII. ON THE GREAT RIVER AND THE ARKANSAS

Very soon after he resigned his mission in June, 1818, Mr. Flint was taken ill and had the long sickness to which reference has already been made.   He was unconscious for thirty days.[181]   Mr. Giddings visited him at the end of August and says:

> Mr. Flint has a severe turn of sickness.   For about four days the physicians did not think he would live from one day to another.   His life was despaired of.   He is mending or was the last I heard from him.   I saw him about two days after his fever abated.   He appeared much resigned, and said he thought he had enjoyed much of the presence of God during his sickness but appeared confident that he should not recover.[182]

In this letter, Mr. Giddings reports that they had organized a church at St. Charles on the twenty-ninth of August, two days after their Presbytery met.   He named the eight people who formed the church and remarks that the step had the entire approbation of Mr. Flint.   He says also that the people of the St. Charles church told him, at the time their church was formed, that they would no longer consider themselves under Mr. Flint's care.[183]   It appears however, that the local prejudice against Mr. Flint was rapidly passing, and that it was a case of "Ill-will" and "Pre-

---

[181] Letter of Timothy Flint, St. Charles, Jan. 15, 1822.
[182] Letter of S. Giddings, St. Louis, Sept. 20, 1818.
[183] — *Idem.*

judice" pouring dirt on "Mr. Goodman." It seems most probable that Mr. Flint continued to preach in St. Charles, after his recovery and until he left for the south. While he was preparing to go down the Mississippi, a subscription for him, as pastor of the church, was started and so liberally supported, that he says it would have induced him, together with other considerations, to have remained in St. Charles, had he known it in time.[184]

St. Charles was one of the places which had strong attractions for Mr. Flint. There was a high bench above the tow looking far over the valley and prairie, and a f rorite place of meditation. He had often thought to inish his career here, and had found the place where he hoped his ashes would rest. There were some very warm friends in the community and the place had become home to the wanderers.[185]

Mr. Flint had for several months been in correspondence with people in the south about church and school work. As early as August, 1817, he had an invitation from "Rapide on Red river." He had also at this time an invitation to go to Alabama, and another to go to Washington, near Natchez, Mississippi. Two things were pulling him, the hope of adequate support, and a populous "country in a religious point of view unexplored."[186] This last place was finally decided upon, but the journey could not

184 Flint. *Recollections*, 215, 216.

185 — *Idem.* Also letter from St. Charles, Jan. 15, 1822.

Bryan and Rose's *Pioneer Families of Missouri* has an interesting and complimentary sketch of Mr. Flint which seems to be made from local traditions. It speaks of his opening a farm on the Marais Croche Lake where he raised cotton and made wine from wild grapes.

186 Letter of Timothy Flint, St. Charles, Aug. 3, 1817.

begin in the fall of 1818 as they had intended, because
of the sickness and slow recovery of Mr. Flint.

In April, 1819, they were ready to depart for the
low country. It was a "solemn leave" that they took
of their home and friends.[187] Three years' residence
in a new community go farther toward the making of
a home than double that time can do in an older society. And this family was a home-loving one, though
they were never to know a place as their own, while
Mr. Flint lived, for more than a few years at a time.

The family embarked upon a very large keelboat
with an ignorant patron. They met with disaster
upon disaster from the first of their journey. Only a
few miles down the river, at Bellefountaine, they ran
aground, and were extricated by the help of a file of
soldiers from the garrison. At the mouth of the Missouri they were carried among the sawyers and nar-
rowly escaped wreck. We were he says, "like to be
sunk in the harbor at St. Louis by a leak in the bottom
of our boat, which commenced in a dark and stormy
night." Opposite "Flour Island" they were struck
by an unusually severe storm which wrecked, in their
sight, two other boats and drowned the occupants.
Their boat was old and frail and its escape at this time,
and a few days later "opposite the middle Chickasaw
bluff," when it was caught in an eddy of the swollen
river and almost broken in two, seemed miraculous.
In this eddy a few days earlier a boat had been broken
and wrecked. They were witnesses of a fourth
wreck before they had reached the mouth of the Arkansas, five hundred miles down the Mississippi. It

187 Letter of Jan. 15, 1822.

was again proving itself the "wicked-river" as the boatmen called it.[188]

On the fifth of May they reached the White River in Arkansas. Mr. Flint says of this event in his *Recollections:*

> We were swept round by the strong current of the Mississippi in our keel-boat between two green islands covered with rushes and cotton-wood trees, into a small bay which received the waters of White River. This is all a region of deep and universal inundation. There was from six to ten feet water over all the bottoms; and we had a wide display of that spectacle so common in the spring on the Mississippi, a dense forest of the largest trees, vocal with the song of birds, matted with every species of tangled vegetation, and harboring in great numbers the turkey-buzzard, and some species of eagles; and all this vegetation apparently rising from the bosom of dark and discolored waters. I have never seen a deeper forest except of evergreens.

The waters of the White River were so clear that they could see the great catfishes among the smaller fishes of all kinds. But no baited hook could tempt them.[189]

From the White River they soon passed by a cross channel to the Arkansas River. They had planned to go up this river to the "Post" some fifty miles distant by water, and leave a consignment of tracts and Bibles which they had for the new territory. They were met at the point where they struck the Arkansas River, or near there, by some prominent people of the "Post" who persuaded them to try this place as a location for their mission. Mrs. Flint was sick at the time and they had enough of experience in these new regions to know that it would be well to go to the south by

---

[188] Flint. *Recollections*, 217-219, also *letter* from St. Charles, Jan. 15, 1822.
[189] Flint. *Recollections*, 252-254.

stages.[190] So it was decided to spend at least the first summer at the "Post" before continuing to Natchez.

Mr. Flint noticed that the Arkansas River marked the border of a new climate.[191] The river itself interested him greatly. He speaks of its reddish waters, the narrow strips of land which formed the banks on either side and through which, during the high waters, the river poured at frequent intervals into the swamps and lagoons which flanked it. These bayous and lagoons he found conforming to the curves of the river, and when they were full during the spring floods, they had a current moving with the river. They were often thirty miles in width. In summer they were covered with a great lily-like flower, the leaves of which completely covered the water in many places. Great forests stretched over most of these flooded regions.[192]

The curves or bends in this river, which it has in common with other rivers of the region, were features of much interest and speculation to Mr. Flint. He thought their regularity must be the result of some unknown law.[193] The upper regions of the river, which however, he did not visit since he did not go, so far as can be discovered, more than one hundred miles above the "Post," were also places of much interest to him. He had studied the reports of travelers about the habits of the river in its upper courses, how it issues from the mountains a clear and rapid stream, and upon the plains loses itself in the sands.

[190] Letter of Timothy Flint, St. Charles, Jan. 15, 1822.
[191] Flint. *Recollections*, 256.
[192] — *Idem*, 256, 264 ff.
[193] — *Idem*, 264, 265.

His prophecy about these sandy plains through which the Arkansas flows is interesting in view of the late developments in that region. Here where the river loses itself in the burning and shifting sands he thinks the buffalo, elk, and bear will range until they "will in ages to come be the resorts of shepherds." [194] "Providence," he thinks, "seems to have provided that men can hardly subsist among them." Here on these vast and sandy plains will be for ages the "Syrtes of America." [195] In the midst of these sandy regions are now some of the most valuable and productive lands of the whole country, yielding not merely the wild grape of which Mr. Flint had heard more than we now know, but fruits of many kinds, sugar beets, melons, and vegetables, besides many farm products, in an amazing abundance, while the entire region had long been occupied by the cattle men with their vast herds before it was used by the farmer. Mr. Flint occasionally indulged in prophecy and in some instances he has come surprisingly near the facts as they have been realized in history. [196] In the case of the upper Arkansas regions he has gone farther astray than is usual with him.

The cypress tree attracted his special notice among the trees of the lower Arkansas country. It constituted a vast proportion of the swamp forests, growing always in water, covered with a thick coat of green, buff, velvet-like matter, while the trees themselves were covered with long moss, or "Spanish beard."

[194] Flint. *Recollections*, 268.
[195] — *Idem*, 255, 256.
[196] See *Western Monthly Review*, vol. i, 255-263.

Concerning the effect of these forests on the observer
he says:

> No prospect on earth can be more gloomy. The poetic Styx
> or Acheron had not a greater union of dismal circumstances.
> Well may the cypress have been esteemed a funereal and lugu-
> brious tree.[197]

The "Post" of Arkansas [Arkansas Post], they
found a rough frontier settlement on a narrow ridge
of land rising out of the Arkansas.   In front of it was
the river and at the back a swamp which was tributary to the White River thirty miles distant.   This
ridge was but six hundred yards wide and about ten
feet above high water.   The entire population of the
territory, which was only about ten thousand at this
time, was settled at a few points along the rivers.[198]

Mr. Flint was in Arkansas only five months and did
not have the opportunities for travel that he had in
Missouri, but in this short time he visited several
points up and down the Arkansas River, and, apparently, the higher country to the north.[199]

He found the territorial legislature enacting "what
they would call 'the blue laws' of old Virginia," and
on the succeeding Sabbath the legislators and judges
would fall to their usual vocation of gambling
throughout the day.[200]

He says of the inhabitants:

> The people of this region are certainly more rough and un-
> tamed than those of the state of Missouri, or of the more north-
> ern and western regions.   But yet, even the inhabitants here were
> far from deserving the character that has generally been given to

[197] Flint. *Recollections*, 261-263.   [199] — *Idem*, 265-267.
[198] — *Idem*, 264, 265.   [200] — *Idem*, 269.

the best of the population of these countries. The redeeming influence of American feelings, laws, and institutions, was sufficiently infused into the new government to carry it into quiet effect throughout the country.[201]

Mr. Flint thought there was no other country which could show such bigotry and enthusiasm, run to such glaring absurdity. He visited and studied carefully a sect known as the "Pilgrims" which had started in Lower Canada and come to the end of its course, with but six persons left, near the "Post" in Arkansas. They had been going southwest to find the New Jerusalem, and at this point had found the fever which had put an end to their search for the Heavenly City on earth. Their principle was the forsaking of the world. Their practice was never to change their clothes, wash themselves, or follow an occupation. Their chant, when entering a village was, "Praise God, repent, fast, pray." Mr. Flint's description of the sect extends through several pages of the *Recollections*, and is worth the notice of students of religious fads.[202]

Mr. Flint's experience in preaching here was one of the most trying he was ever called upon to endure in his capacity as a minister. The services were held in the Court House. There were no religious habits, and he felt that his few sermons had but little effect. Some emotion was visible, but he felt that his mission was like that of the itinerants, and that both his and their work was like the fire that passes over a stubble field, lightly, and which in a few days leaves no sign of its presence.[203]

[201] Flint. *Recollections*, 269, 270.   [203] — *Idem*, 274.
[202] — *Idem*, 275-280.

At this time Mr. Flint was preaching in French, though his pronunciation was defective, because most of his audience was of that nation. He says of these hearers:

> The French people generally came to the place of worship, arrayed in their ball-dresses, and went directly from worship to the ball. A billiard-room was near, and parts of my audience sometimes came in for a moment, and after listening to a few sentences, returned to their billiards.[204]

This last experience he had at other places as well.

While he was one hundred miles up the river, probably at the Mulberry settlement, in July, his family was taken sick with the epidemic fever of the country. All of them were seized except Mr. Flint. A negro child died in his family. His hired negro servant was taken sick and he could get no one else. The only doctor they could trust, a member of his family at the time, was sick also. Mrs. Flint and Micah were so ill as to be thought hopeless. There were a great many deaths all about them. For sixty days Mr. Flint says, he was nurse, physician, and housekeeper.[205]

It was at this time that they suffered from a hurricane. His journal and other manuscripts were lost. He says:

> This manuscript, together with many others, was blown away in a hurricane which occurred on the Arkansas, in which every part of the house where we resided was penetrated by the wind and rain; and in which the suffering and danger of a sick family precluded anxiety upon any other score.[206]

It was during this summer too, that the family ex-

---

[204] Flint. *Recollections*, 274.

[205] — *Idem*, 271, 272. Also letter from St. Charles, Jan. 15, 1822.

[206] Flint. *Recollections*, 4.

perienced drenching rain and thunder storms for thirty-six days in succession.[207]

Added to these larger afflictions was a lesser one that ought not to be entirely overlooked, and will not be by any one who has had anything of a similar experience. It was the pest of mosquitoes. The natives had grown somewhat accustomed to it though they excused their heavy drinking by the necessity they were under of thus gaining relief from the miseries caused by this pest. They called the reverie or the insensibility of drunkenness "a musquitoe dose." The Flints could not eat a meal at their table all that summer without first kindling a fire under the table, out of the most offensive materials. Of his experiences at night Flint says:

> I slept under a very close mosquito curtain. I would soon become oppressed for want of breath under the curtain, and when I drew it up and attempted to inhale a little of the damp and sultry atmosphere, the mosquitoes would instantly settle on my face in such numbers that I was soon obliged to retreat behind my curtain again. Thus passed those dreadful nights, amidst the groans of my family, calls for medicine and drink, suffocation behind my curtain, or the agony of mosquito stings, as soon as I was exposed to the air.[208]

Mr. Flint tells us in the letter to the Missionary Society, that under the conditions of their summer in Arkansas the entire family came to have an aversion to the low country and thought only of getting back to the north. As early as possible, and while Mrs. Flint had still to be carried, they took boat and started to return to St. Charles, in the early part of October, 1819. Boatmen often failed them and Mr. Flint was

[207] Flint. *A condensed Geography and History*, vol. i, 582.
[208] Flint. *Recollections*, 272, 273.

obliged to handle the boat with the help of his three children who still had the ague and were sick every other day.[209] Near the mouth of the Arkansas, at St. Francis, they stopped with Mr. Phillips, an acquaintance, who pressed them to remain with him until the river should be higher next spring. At this season it was so low that there were almost no boats upon the river, all steamboats being laid up. Mr. Flint desired to stay but Mrs. Flint and the family were so anxious to leave the country that it was decided to go on.[210]

As this was to be the saddest journey of all that this long suffering family experienced, it will be quite in place to notice its joys. It was a beautiful fall. Nature was at her best, most wild and beautiful. The paroxysms of ague, when they were passed, left a kind of poetic excitement, not unlike that produced by opium, and making one capable of a high degree of enjoyment. Mr. Flint gives us a picture of one of these nights:

> Then, when we were made fast in a cove on the wide sand-bar; when the moon, with her circumference broadened and reddened by the haze and smoke of Indian summer, rose, and diffused, as Chateaubriand so beautifully says, the "great secret of melancholy over these ancient forests;" after our evening prayers, and the favorite hymn, "The day is past and gone," etc. I have spent hours in traversing the sand-bars entirely alone.[211]

Progress up the river was very slow. They had not gone far before their two "hands" fell ill and left Mr. Flint and the two boys, to drag the six ton boat up the river. Some days the boys were sick with the ague

---

[209] Letter of Timothy Flint, St. Charles, Jan. 15, 1822.
[210] Flint. *Recollections*, 283.
[211] — *Idem*, 285.

and the father toiled alone at the cordelle. The
boat would lodge on sandbars and he would have to go
into the water and push it off though the ice was at
times strong enough along the shore to bear his
weight.[212] They toiled at one place for two or three
days and were about to lay by for the winter when a
fortunate wind aided them with their sail to go on.
They exhausted their provisions, and were at the point
of hunger when they sighted a boat loaded with flour
and pork. They were compelled to pay thirty dollars
for a barrel of each, the boatmen discovering and taking advantage of their plight.[213]

When they had accomplished two hundred miles of
their journey up the Mississippi, and were "opposite
the second Chickasaw bluff," at a point called "Rare
Paths" and thirty miles from human habitation, on the
twenty-sixth of November, there occurred the most
touching incident that is possible in the experience of
a Christian family. Mr. Flint tells the story at length
in the *Recollections*,[214] and more briefly but with a few
additional details in his letter to the Missionary Society.[215] Flint says:

> At ten in the morning we perceived indications of a severe
> approaching storm. The air was oppressively sultry. Brassy
> clouds were visible upon all quarters of the sky. Distant thun-
> der was heard. We were upon a wide sandbar far from any
> house. Opposite to us was a vast cypress swamp. At this pe-
> riod, and in this place, Mrs. F. was taken in travail. My children,
> wrapped in blankets, laid themselves down on the sand-bar. I
> secured the boat in every possible way against the danger of being

[212] Letter of Timothy Flint, St. Charles, Jan. 15, 1822.
[213] Flint. *Recollections*, 285, 286.
[214] See pages 286-288.
[215] Jan. 15, 1822.

driven by the storm into the river. At eleven the storm burst upon us in all its fury. Mrs. F. had been salivated during her fever, and had not yet been able to leave her couch. I was alone with her in this dreadful situation. Hail, and wind, and thunder, and rain in torrents poured upon us. I was in terror, lest the wind would drive my boat, notwithstanding all her fastenings, into the river. No imagination can reach what I endured. [Nothing left but God, and He appeared for us. – Letter.] The only alleviating circumstance was her perfect tranquillity. She knew that the hour of sorrow, and expected that of death, was come. She was so perfectly calm, spoke with such tranquil assurance about the future, and about the dear ones that were at this moment, " 'biding the pelting of the pitiless storm" on the sand-bar, that I became calm myself. A little after twelve the wind burst in the roof of my boat, and let in the glare of the lightning, and the torrents of rain upon my poor wife. I could really have expostulated with the elements in the language of the poor old Lear. I had wrapped my wife in blankets, ready to be carried to the shelter of the forest, in case of the driving of my boat into the river. About four the fury of the storm began to subside. At five the sun in his descending glory burst from the dark masses of the receding clouds. At eleven in the evening Mrs. F. was safely delivered of a female infant, and, notwithstanding all, did well. The babe, from preceding circumstances, was feeble and sickly, and I saw could not survive. At midnight we had raised a blazing fire. The children came into the boat. Supper was prepared, and we surely must have been ungrateful not to have sung a hymn of deliverance. There can be but one trial more for me that can surpass the agony of that day, and there can never be on this earth a happier period than those midnight hours. The babe stayed with us but two days and a half, and expired. The children, poor things, laid it deeply to heart, and raised a loud lament. We were, as I have remarked, far away from all human aid and sympathy, and left alone with God. We deposited the body of our lost babe – laid in a small trunk for a coffin – in a grave amidst the rushes, there to await the resurrection of the dead. The prayer made on the occasion by the father, with the children for concourse and mourners, if not eloquent, was, to us at least, deeply affecting.

The grave was made on a high bank opposite to "the second Chickasaw bluff," a rude memorial was raised on the spot and the place became sacred in the memories of the devoted family. Micah, some years later, wrote "Lines on Passing the Grave of My Sister." It was published in the *Western Monthly Review*,[216] and will be found in Appendix C.

---

[216] See vol. i, 651-653.

VIII. PREACHING AND FARMING IN MISSOURI

After the pathetic incident related at the close of the last chapter, the Flint family proceeded on their painful and sorrowful journey up the river. They were fortunate enough to secure two men to aid them at this time, but after two weeks more of travel, when they had reached the southern line of Missouri, the ice began to hinder them, and the weather grew severe. These difficulties together with the fact that their boat, though it drew but thirty inches of water, was continually striking on the sand bars, led them to land at New Madrid, with the intention of completing their journey by land.[217] But St. Charles was still more than two hundred miles distant, they were yet feeble from their recent sicknesses, and the season and region most unfavorable for such a journey to be undertaken by a family.

This village of New Madrid was not so wretched and abandoned a place as Mr. Flint had expected to find it. There were some rare people there, who, when the Flints came to know them and to experience their kindliness and hospitality, were remembered ever after as among their choicest friends. This was not only for their work's sake toward the strangers but for their intrinsic worth of character. This place

---

[217] Flint. *Recollections*, 219, 220, 288.

had in past years been the scene of several serious at-
tempts under the Spanish rule, to found a strong colony.   There were some prominent French and American families located here as a result of such an attempt
by a General Morgan of New Jersey.   An elderly
lady, Mrs. Gray, gave the family a part of her house
and here they lived for the winter, from the middle of
December, when they arrived, until the spring or early
summer.[218]

There were several congenial families here, and
with their help Mr. Flint began religious services,
which he considered quite successful, and especially
so as far as the Catholics were concerned.   A Sunday
School was formed apparently at this time, and was
continued under the care of Mrs. Gray for several
years, though Mr. Flint speaks of her as having seen
seventy winters.[219]   It would seem that there were
those here who desired to have Mr. Flint settle as their
minister and that a subscription was raised for that
purpose.   However, the people failed to pay what
they promised and the minister moved on after a few
months, to the county town, Jackson, some fifty miles
up the river.[220]

In New Madrid, Mr. Flint experienced, he says:
"a harrowing degree of interest, in the disappointments and sufferings of these original adventurers,"
many of whom had been reared in all the tenderness
of opulence and plenty, and were from highly cultivated and distinguished French families.[221]

[218] Flint. *Recollections*, 220, 221.
[219] — *Idem*, 220, 228.
[220] Letter of Timothy Flint, St. Charles, Jan. 15, 1822.
[221] Flint. *Recollections*, 221.

There was also another local interest at this place upon which he dwells at much length, namely, the great earthquakes which had occurred seven years before his arrival there, that is, in 1812. This disaster had almost a morbid interest for Mr. Flint as it had of course, for many of those who witnessed it. The original shocks had occurred in two series of concussions. At one time the movement of the earth was vertical. At another time it was horizontal. There were great chasms opened in the earth running from northeast to southwest. Hundreds of these were still visible when Mr. Flint was there. The earth had seemed to burst in other places. Such were the phenomena near New Madrid on the Mississippi River. The result was that the waters were thrown back into the bayous, many boats were wrecked, and others were landed there and abandoned with their cargoes, by their owners. Provisions, in consequence lost almost all value in the New Madrid district. The bed of the river was changed at different points. Lakes were made and unmade. For a distance of three hundred miles below New Madrid the face of the country was changed in many striking ways. The cemetery on a high point of land overlooking the river at New Madrid had been cast into the river. The town had been largely depopulated, and many houses, with orchards and farms were still abandoned at the time even of Mr. Flint's visit. No buildings had been erected after the earthquakes except the lightest kind.[222]

As the people grew more experienced with the dan-

[222] Flint. *Recollections*, 222-228.

gers, a unique plan of deliverance from the opening
chasms in the earth, was hit upon. The tallest trees
were felled to the northwest and the southeast, at
right angles to the direction in which the chasms
opened. When the earthquake premonitions were
heard, the people hurried to their felled trees. Mr.
Flint says, that by this means all were saved though
openings often occurred under the tree trunks on
which the people were mounted.[223]

The government came to the aid of the stricken
people and allowed them to locate on public lands in
other sections in place of ruined or abandoned farms
in the devastated district.[224]

Several strange phenomena are reported by Mr.
Flint. There were said to have been continued and
vivid flashes of lightning in the western sky on perfectly clear nights, in the intervals between the earthquake shocks. There were at such times, subterra-
nean thunders. The worst of these was thought to
have been on the night in which the fatal earthquakes
at Caracas, Venezuela, occurred. Birds and animals
were said to have fled in terror to the people for pro-
tection. Where the earth burst, water, sand, and pit-
coal were hurled in great volumes as high as the tops
of the trees.[225]

Occasional shocks had been felt during the seven
years. While they sat by Mrs. Gray's winter fire, he
says:

We were not unfrequently interrupted for a moment by the

---

[223] Flint. *Recollections*, 226.
[224] — *Idem*, 227. Letter of S. Giddings, St. Louis, March 21, 1818.
[225] — *Idem*, 223, 224.

distant and hollow thunder of the approaching earthquake.   An
awe, a slight paleness passed over every countenance.   The narrative was suspended for a moment, and resumed.[226]

Little is told about the year or more, that the Flint
family spent in Jackson, Missouri.*   He was engaged
in preaching and did much traveling.   There was
considerable talk among the German people for whom
he preached a part or all of this time about liberal pay,
but after he had left that section and returned to St.
Charles he said that he had received nothing but
promises for his services as minister.   He and the
family earned their living by their labor and had
managed to keep out of debt.[227]   From references that
he makes to German pupils, though he does not say
where he had them, and from the fact that the school
was always so closely related to their missionary work
and so sure a means of helping to make a living, it is
altogether likely that this was a part of their work
here.   It is also likely that some farming was done.
The oldest son was in his eighteenth year and the second son, Hubbard, was twelve or thirteen years old at
this time.

Flint says about his time spent in Jackson that it was
"more devoid of interest, or of attachment, or comfort,
or utility, than in any other part of the country."   He
says:

> The people are extremely rough.   Their country is a fine
> range for all species of sectarians, furnishing the sort of people in
> abundance, who are ignorant, bigoted, and think, by devotion to

---

[226] Flint. *Recollections*, 229.

* For this period in Flint's travels see Houck's *History of Missouri*, vol.
iii, 232.

[227] Letter of Timothy Flint, St. Charles, Jan. 15, 1822.

some favored preacher or sect, to atone for the want of morals and decency, and everything that appertains to the spirit of Christianity.[228]

It is of this section that Mr. Flint speaks especially when he makes one of his most interesting remarks on the religious character of the western people. He says:

> They are anxious to collect a great many people and preachers, and achieve, if the expression may be allowed, a great deal of religion at once, that they may lie by, and be exempt from its rules and duties until the regular recurrence of the period for replenishing the stock. Hence we witness the melancholy aspect of much appearance and seeming, frequent meetings, spasms, cries, fallings, faintings, and, what I imagine will be a new aspect of religious feeling to most of my readers, the religious laugh. Nothing is more common at these scenes, than to see the more forward people on these occasions indulging in what seemed to me an idiot and spasmodic laugh, and when I asked what it meant, I was told it was the holy laugh! Preposterous as the term may seem to my readers, the phrase "holy laugh" is so familiar to me, as no longer to excite surprise. But in these same regions, and among these same people, morals, genuine tenderness of heart, and capacity to be guided either by reason, persuasion, or the uniform dictates of the gospel, was an affecting desideratum.[229]

The scene of Mr. Flint's *George Mason* is probably laid here in Missouri, rather than in Mississippi, where he has located it in the story. He never resided in the latter state. The trying experiences of the New England minister's family under the name of the Masons must tell much of what the Flints felt and suffered keenly from, in the rude society of Jackson, and other places as well. Mr. Flint would not give expression to it in his letters or in his *Recollections*. It was a part of the many things that he withheld not

[228] Flint. *Recollections*, 232.   [229] — *Idem*, 238, 239.

"blazoning" them even to his friends.[230]   In the story of *George Mason* we see how the poverty of the New England family is despised by the rich planters, how their modesty and reticence is taken for pride, and how their unwillingness to conform to the rude religious and social customs of their neighbors leads to their ostracism and even persecution.   The sons of the two wealthiest planters fall in love with the twelve year old daughter of the New England family and in their frontier way proceeded to woo her despite the protests of mother and daughter, that she was only a child.   [Mr. Flint's daughter Emeline was about fifteen when they lived in Jackson.]   In the south that age was considered quite old enough for courtship and marriage.   The author remarks that he had frequently seen mothers but fourteen years of age.

While at Jackson, Mr. Flint was much interested in the nearby German settlement on the Whitewater River.   These people were from Pennsylvania, North Carolina, and Germany direct.   They were settled in the forests and very much isolated both by their habits and location.   Flint thought they had preserved their nationality better even than their countrymen in Pennsylvania.   Indeed he remarks about this time that he thinks all the Europeans, and the Anglo-Americans as well, are far more devoted to their national and state habits after they have once lost themselves in this new world.   Much of the infelicity of society in the new country he says came from this clannishness, aggravated by the strange surroundings and the latent homesickness of the people.[231]   He has

230 Letter of Timothy Flint, St. Charles, Jan. 15, 1822.
231 Flint. *Recollections*, 244.

no fear but that this marked trait of the early western society will pass and all will be proud to be a part of the nation that is soon to be a recognized power in the family of nations.[232]

The Germans, he considered the most prosperous class of people in the west. The French seemed to him the least so. The very appearance of many of them, "spare, thin, sallow, and tanned, with their flesh adhering to their bones, and apparently dried to the consistency of parchment" was in striking and eloquent contrast to the "large, stout, and ruddy-looking men and women," in the German settlements. As a race the French did not rise above indigence, while the Germans were generally independent and often rich. Everything about their farms had the appearance of permanence and strength. Their cattle and horses were large. He said:

> They spend little, and when they sell will receive nothing in pay but specie. Every stroke counts towards improvement. Their wives have no taste for parties and tea. Silent, unwearied labor, and the rearing of their children, are their only pursuits; and in a few years they are comparatively rich.

The French were "a poor race of hunters, crowded in villages with mud hovels, fond of conversation and coffee." Next to the Germans in prosperity were the Anglo-Americans, then the Scotch, while the direct emigrants from England were only more successful than the French.[233]

Mr. Flint found his German parishioners anxious for religious instruction and devoted to the German ideals of honesty and industry, though they had one great weakness. He says:

---

[232] Flint. *Recollections*, 252.   [233] — *Idem*, 237.

But almost every farmer has his distillery, and the pernicious poison, whiskey, dribbles from the corn; and in their curious dialect, they told me, that while they wanted religion, and their children baptized, and a minister as exemplary as possible, he must allow the honest Dutch, as they call themselves, to partake of the native beverage. And they undertook to prove that the swearing and drunkenness of a Dutchman was not so bad as that of an American. One of them was reproved for his intemperance and profaneness, and it was remarked that he had been zealous and very strict in his religious profession in Carolina. "Never mind," said he, "this is a bad country for religion. I know that I have lost him," he continued, "but never mind, by and by the good breacher," as he phrased it, "will come along, and I shall pick him all up again.[234]

These people had brought a minister named Weiberg with them to the country. He was an educated man but a notorious drunkard. Says Mr. Flint:

The earnest manner in which he performed divine service in their own ritual [the Lutheran] and in their own language, carried away all their affections. . . After service he would get drunk, and as often happens among them, was quarrelsome. They claimed indulgence to get drunk themselves, but were not quite so clear in allowing their minister the same privilege.

When the time came to pay their subscriptions they refused on the ground of his failing. Three successive years he sued for and recovered his salary. And

To reinstate himself in their good will, it was only necessary for him to take them when a sufficient quantity of whiskey had opened their phlegmatic natures to sensibility, and then give them a vehement discourse, as they phrased it, in the pure old Dutch, and give them a German hymn of his own manufacture, for he was a poet, too, and the subscription paper was once more brought forward. They who had lost their suit and had been most inveterate in their dislike, were thawed out, and crowded about the paper either to sign their name or make their mark.[235]

---

[234] Flint. *Recollections*, 233.   [235] — *Idem*, 234, 235.

But the Reverend Herr Weiberg had finally been banished to a neighboring German colony and the Yankee "Breacher" was in his place.

He occasionally returned to Germany as it was called, to taste their whiskey and cider. . . He came to the house of Madam Ballinger, where I usually stayed when among them. "Well," said he, "I judge you will now get good fast, now that you have a Yankee breacher. Does he know one word of Dutch?" "Very little, I suppose," she replied; but in order to vindicate her preacher, she added, "but he knows French," etc., and she went on giving my knowledge of various languages, according to her own fancy: "And, mein Gott, what I tinks much good, he does not drink one trop of whiskey!" [236]

Mr. Flint says further about his German congregation,

I had the good fortune to be very acceptable to this people, although I could not smoke, drink whiskey, nor talk German. They made various efforts to fix my family among them. And, as the highest expression of good will, they told me that they would do more than they had done for Weiberg. [237]

Whether it was because the "Yankee breacher"

[236] The funeral customs of these German people may be of interest. Flint says — "I attended a funeral, where there were a great number of them present. After I had performed such services as I was used to perform on such occasions, a most venerable looking old man, of the name of Nyeswinger, with a silver beard that flowed down his chin, came forward and asked me if I were willing that he should perform some of their peculiar rites. I of course wished to hear them. He opened a very ancient version of Luther's hymns, and they began to sing in German, so loud that the woods echoed the strain; and yet there was something affecting in the singing of these ancient people, carrying one of their brethren to his long home, in the use of the language and rites which they had brought with them over the sea from the 'fader land,' a word which often occurred in their hymn. It was a long, loud, and mournful air, which they sung as they bore the body along. The words 'mein Gott,' 'mein broder,' and 'fader land,' died away in the distant woods. Remembrances and associations rushed upon me, and I shall long remember that funeral hymn." — *Recollections*, 235, 236.

[237] Flint. *Recollections*, 236.

could not meet them in more of their social customs, whether it was because he would not pursue Weiberg's method of collecting his salary and renewing the subscriptions, is not known. It is clear, however, that the promises and efforts amounted to nothing; and early in September, 1821, after spending almost two years in southern Missouri, the family started overland for St. Charles.[238]

On this one hundred and fifty mile journey they probably had some heavy conveyance which would carry their household effects and the mother and infant. For, during this summer, a fifth child (the fourth to live) was born to them, on June 8, 1821, at Jackson. He was named James Timothy.[239] Their "Joseph" Mr. Flint calls him. He was to be their comfort indeed in after years.

This journey to St. Charles would lead them by a way that was not as strange as all their former paths in a new country. There would be friends and acquaintances at Ste. Genevieve. There were the Hempsteads and many others at St. Louis. The journey was leisurely for they did not reach St. Charles until about the middle of October.[240]

Their former farm home below St. Charles had been sold when they left in the spring of 1819. Still they felt that there they were at home. Mr. Flint says in the letter to the Missionary Society, January 15, 1822, that their welcome had been very cordial from their former friends in St. Charles, and that he

---

[238] Letter of Timothy Flint, St. Charles, Jan. 15, 1822.

[239] Family Records. Manuscripts in Boston Public Library and Library of Harvard University.

[240] Letter of Timothy Flint, St. Charles, Jan. 15, 1822.

had obtained a perpetual lease on a farm four miles
from St. Charles, having "determined to farm for
subsistence, and to preach altogether gratis." This
farm must have been below the village and near where
their former home had been. In the *Recollections*,[241] he makes acknowledgment of special indebt-
edness to two families who lived below St. Charles at
the "Point."

The letter continues:

> We began with some degree of cheerfulness to build our cabin,
> where we expected to end our days. The second day of our
> labor, we were all struck in one day with the dreadful fever of the
> country. We were penniless and homeless. For more than 30
> days, all consciousness and remembrance was lost to me. The
> neighbors took Mrs. F. and me to one house, our daughter was
> carried to another. Mrs. F. had an infant and it was taken from
> the breast, and carried to another place. My two boys had but a
> slight attack, and went to another place. The first of January
> we were all re-assembled in the cabin, where we now live, but all
> afflicted with the ague, which has now followed me seventy days.

The *Recollections* adds some details to the story of
this sad homecoming. In the height of his fever, circumstances made it necessary for Mr. Flint to be removed from the house where he was taken sick.
While he was unable to raise himself in bed, he was
moved in a carriage to a house six miles distant. He
writes:

> Sick as we were and probable as the prospect was, that some of
> us would add the trouble of funeral rites and duties to the labor
> and cares of nursing us, they never remitted their kindness for a
> moment.

He is not permitted to name these friends, but as
he looks back upon those dreary days, writing a few

---

[241] **Page 190.**

Presbyterian Church, St. Charles, Missouri

Built *about* 1819

years later, probably in Salem, or perhaps at the parental home in North Reading, he says:

> How often, when thinking of these families, to whom we owe so much, have I remembered Gray's beautiful verses – "Full many a gem," etc.[242]

By the first of the year, 1822, the cabin had been completed, and probably much earlier for the two boys, as we have seen, were not seriously ill. There was another trouble, however, for the missionary letter says:

> We are now for the first time in debt. [He probably means debt as a result of living expenses and sickness.] I have no apparent means of payment – for I am utterly incapable of assisting my family, and Mrs. Flint has the ague sometimes many days in succession. Under these circumstances, we are discouraged with the country. Our industry, we think, would avail us more in a healthier climate. The people of St. Charles have shown great kindness, but our situation is still sufficiently wretched. We seem to have no prospect here, but to wear out with continual fever and ague. Our friends at the eastward propose to assist us in some small degree, to return to Mass. Perhaps your society, which assisted us to come here, will compassionate our case, and join our friends in aiding us to return. Any of the Missionaries here will inform you that instead of blazoning our misfortunes, we have kept the greater part of them back. Perhaps your society will think it as meritorious, to assist a distressed, and worn out family to revisit their friends – as to fit the fresh Miss. out.[243]

Mr. Flint was an honorable and independent man, and his putting aside his pride to write the above letter would not be the least of his sufferings. He would not have done it at all but for the helpless family, which he was not then able to do anything for, and for which he seemed unlikely to be able to provide

---

[242] Page 191.
[243] Letter of Timothy Flint, St. Charles, Jan. 15, 1822.

in that section. Certainly none will dare to charge him with anything of the pauper spirit in this instance until they have entered into some sympathy with the desperate situation in which his family was at this time placed.

Hear him a little farther, though one shrinks from making public even at this day what cost a brother, as this cost Mr. Flint. He writes:

You can easily conceive the strong repugnance, which I feel at making a proposal so humiliating to our natural feelings. But I may say with the catholic church, "e profundis exclamavi."

I have looked upon my family, and all pride has sunk within me. The view of their condition has wrung from me this proposal. I have traveled farther – and have suffered more, and have preached as much – as any Miss. in the country. Should your society see fit to remit me something in aid of my returning next fall, I may, perhaps, see you, and thank you and them in person. At any rate you will not censure this my proposal until you have placed yourselves in my situation in fancy, in an open cabin, one or the other still groaning with the ague – and no resource, but the casual kindness of a few friends, whom the frequent view of similar cases has rendered callous to them.

I am persuaded, my dear Sir [Reverend Abel Flint, secretary of the Missionary Society of Connecticut] that you will give our case a kind and considerate hearing, and that your delicacy will not expose our case, except there be some prospect of some assistance. Should I survive my present complaint, of which I sometimes doubt, it is doubtful, if I shall ever be able to preach again, though my friends seem anxious, that I should resume my labors here. But whether I recover, or not, whether your society aid me, or not, I am resigned, I am, and shall be personally your affectionate friend, and hum. serv.   T. FLINT.

One feels that the appeal to the Missionary Society of Connecticut was just and proper. It would not seem that anyone who contributed to the funds of the society at that time would have objected to such use of the money when they knew even a small part of the story. But a careful and repeated study of the Society's list of disbursements for the year 1822 [244] and of the six thousand three hundred, four dollars and sixty-six and one-half cents disbursed by order of the trustees, not one cent went to the Flint family though there were three other missionaries in the new state of Missouri who received a total of four hundred, eighty-five dollars. It ought to be said, however, that aid may very possibly have been sent to Mr. Flint from constituents of the society and through its influence. Such items, probably, would not be officially reported.

---

[244] *Twenty-Fourth Annual Narrative of Missions* (Hartford, 1823) has a statement of the funds for the year 1822.

IX. FLORIDA AND NEW ORLEANS

Whether or not Mr. Flint served the St. Charles church as minister after his recovery in the winter of 1822, and until his departure in October of that year, we are not informed. It is altogether likely that he preached for them at least a part of the time. He and the boys devoted themselves to their farm during the spring and summer.[246]

It is quite probable that during this year Mr. Flint was doing something with his pen, hoping thus to help gain a living and do his part of the world's work. His *George Mason* very likely chronicles something of this year's experiences, as for instance when Mr. Mason is represented as working on a book which he had expected to find time and inspiration to finish, here in his Arcadia. But with the work of clearing a little garden spot in the forest,

The father's hands were one blister. . . The severe toil, too, caused Mr. Mason rheumatic pains and sleepless nights. He found, moreover, when stormy weather confined him to the house, that a body full of the pains of exhausting labor, would not allow scope to his thoughts, when he sat down to his great work with his pen. Unremitting toil, in such a frame, blunts the sensibilities, suspends the exercise of the imagination and fancy, and after a fruitless effort to stir up his thoughts, he was compelled to admit, that severe labor and writing are incompatible.[247]

[246] Flint. *Recollections*, 291.
[247] Flint, Timothy. *George Mason, the Young Backwoodsman*, 32.

It would not be surprising to learn that *George Mason* was written during this year of the second residence in St. Charles.   It would have been more possible than in the busy Cincinnati years just before it was published.

Mr. Flint tells us that they took leave of their friends in St. Charles at this time – the last they were to see of this place of their wanderings – after a sacramental meeting, being he says, "accompanied by the prayers and tears of many friends, not without corresponding tears of our own." [248]

When they were preparing to depart from St. Charles, they had all, apparently, recovered their health.   Their prospects for a living, and for usefulness were not, however, sufficiently bright to encourage them to stay in this section of the west.   It was with the help of eastern friends that they had prepared to return to New England, via the Mississippi and the Atlantic.

Mr. Flint makes a delicate and warm expression of his obligations to the two friends, who, at this period came to his rescue.   He "would tell all" if it were not for the feelings of his family.   His friend, Dr. James Flint, who settled in 1821 as pastor of the East Church, Salem, was one of the friends, and the other we have no doubt, was Joseph Peabody, the Salem merchant. [249]

The journey down the Mississippi was begun the fourth of October, 1822, in company with Mr. William Postell, of St. Charles, who had joined Mr. Flint

[248] Flint. *Recollections*, 217.

[249] — *Idem*, 291, 292. See also the Dedications of the *Recollections* and the *Geography and History*.

in building a flatboat and fitting it up for the use of a family. Two days after they had taken leave of the St. Charles friends, they left the quiet retreat on the prairie below the town. But before they had gotten out of the Missouri they lodged on a sand bar which held them for four days and until they had unloaded their boat. They were not ready to go on until the end of the week. They tied up at St. Louis for the Sabbath. Mr. Flint says of this occasion at St. Louis, "I preached to a very serious audience, a farewell discourse. Many circumstances concurred to give solemnity to this parting." Such partings are always times for reviewing the past. It would not be difficult to enter into some of the concurring circumstances which made this occasion so solemn for people and minister.[250]

After the first mishap on the sandbar in the Missouri, this journey was prosperous all the long way to New Orleans. As far as the Arkansas there was nothing of the charm of novelty which was always so keen with Mr. Flint. There was much of sadness associated with every rapid place in the river and especially with one particular point "opposite the second Chickasaw bluff."

After they have passed below the Arkansas, Mr. Flint begins in his *Recollections* a history of the settlements which they pass, the new aspects of the vegetable world as it grows more tropical, the different appearance of the forests, and especially the difference in the character of the settlements with their increasing number of negro huts and villages about the great planta-

[250] Flint. *Recollections*, 217, 219.

tion buildings.   Much of this material must be valuable for the historian of this period and section.

At Warrenton, Mississippi, just below where Vicksburg now stands, they came to the first village of any size below New Madrid, Missouri.   Here they stopped for a day or two and made inquiries about the religious life and interests of the place.   Though there were a hundred good residences and many brick store buildings in the place, he could find but one person who was known as a professor of religion.   He says:

> I was directed to a young lady, whose husband had something of the appearance of a dandy, and who answered my inquiries about the profession of his wife, with a shrug, and a half-suppressed smile, informing me that she was a Methodist, but would be glad to converse with any person who wore the garb and appearance of a minister.   He gave me clearly to understand that it was no affair of his and that I must converse with her alone. She spoke discouragingly about the willingness of the people to assemble for public worship.   I retired, considering it a hopeless attempt, and intending to pass on without any public exercise. But in the course of the evening a number of the citizens came on board, offering their houses and wishing to have public worship. There was a full house and apparently an attentive audience.

They left this place the next morning after hearing many regrets expressed by the people that in so considerable and prosperous a place there should be so little public spirit and so little religious feeling, as to have no place of public worship.[251]

Natchez they found a romantically situated place which the inhabitants called a city.   It was the principal cotton-shipping point of the region.   At some seasons a thousand boats could be seen at the landing.

---

[251] Flint. *Recollections*, 294, 295.

The lower part of the town, "under the hill," was a repulsive place, the center of all that was vile from the upper and lower country, "the refuse of the world." Of the houses in this section of Natchez, Mr. Flint says: "The fiddle screaks jargon from these *faucibus orci.*" The other part of the town on a bluff three hundred feet high, showed a rich country round about, and it contained many handsome public buildings, on wide streets, with the appearance of comfort and opulence. There was a Baptist, a Methodist and a Presbyterian church,[252] the latter with a large building and society. Mr. Flint had no books at hand as he wrote and estimated the population of Natchez at seven or eight thousand. He notes also that though the town was clean and the air seemingly pure they had repeated and severe visits of the yellow fever.[253]

One hundred and fifty miles above New Orleans they came to the levee on the west side of the river. Another began a little lower on the east side and each continued to New Orleans. They were struck by the high state of cultivation which obtained on the narrow strip of coast land on each side of the river and lying under the levee. This coast land was usually about two miles wide, bounded at the back by the swamps and forests, conforming to the shape of the

[252] Flint. *Recollections*, 295. For the origin of this and other Presbyterian churches in the vicinity, see J. G. Jones's *A Concise History of the Introduction of Protestantism into Mississippi and the Southwest*, 225-238. Mr. Jones says the first Protestant church in this section, and so far as the writer can learn it was the first church with a settled pastor west of the Alleghany Mountains, was a Congregational church at Kingston, Miss. It was formed by Reverend Samuel Swayze, and a colony from New Jersey in 1872 or 1873.

[253] Flint. *Recollections*, 295, 296.

river, and very rich. Sounds heard from the houses
below them seemed to come from beneath the river.
The houses and grounds were very beautiful and Mr.
Flint thought that no other section of the Union, not
even the banks of the Delaware could compare for
fertility and productiveness with this section. Among
the noblest of the plantations that they saw was that
of General Hampton, "one of the questionable heroes
of the late war," Mr. Flint thinks.[254]

In all this marvelously rich and beautiful section of
country, with its dense population, Mr. Flint was
pained to find no Protestant church, though the eye
was cheered by the sight of a Catholic spire every six
or seven miles. He thought it hardly necessary to go
to Hindustan to find whole regions destitute of even
the forms of Christian worship. At Baton Rouge
they admired the United States barracks which Mr.
Flint thought as commodious as any in the whole
country. The two or three companies of troops were
under high discipline. There was a beautiful white
monument on the grounds, erected in honor of some
officers of the garrison who had died there, but the
inscription on it seemed to Mr. Flint a reproach in a
professedly Christian country. As he remembered
the verse it was:

> Like bubbles on a sea of matter borne,
> We rise, we burst, and to that sea return.[255]

We are not told just when the Flint party reached
New Orleans, but it was probably some time in November and in the healthiest season. Their health
must have been so much improved and the country so

---

254 Flint. *Recollections*, 297, 300.   255 — *Idem*, 299, 300.

attractive in various ways that they were in no hurry to proceed to New England and so complete the long journey they had begun. In January of that winter, Mr. Flint tells us that he ascended the river on a steamboat as far as Baton Rouge. He does not tell us the object of this trip but devotes a page or two of the *Recollections* to what he saw at that time.[256] They spent about four months in New Orleans during the first winter's residence there and at New Year's time were enjoying peas in bloom, daffodils, and roses.[257] Mr. Flint spent part of the time gathering material for his *Geography and History* in the French manuscripts in the archives of state.[258]

The Flints had friends in the south to welcome them. These, with new and influential ones, desired to locate them permanently in this section of the country. In this way they became interested in Covington, thirty-five miles north of New Orleans, and across Lake Pontchartrain. Mr. Flint repeatedly calls this section West Florida although it was then, and had been since 1810, claimed by the United States as a part of Louisiana. In 1812, it was made a part of the state of Louisiana, and in 1819 and 1821, all possible claim of Spain upon it had been surrendered to the United States.[259]

On a stormy March evening they embarked on a steamer that was to carry them across this broad and shallow lake for the scene of their new labors. So low were its shores and so wide its shallow waters that

[256] In the year 1823; pages 299, 300.

[257] *Western Monthly Review*, vol. iii, 633.

[258] — *Idem*, vol. i, opposite 128. Also *Geography and History*, vol. i, 13.

[259] Channing, E. *The Jeffersonian System*, map, opp. 142.

in its center it was difficult or even impossible to see
land, though it was only thirty miles wide. When
the water was rough the surf broke far in the forests
so low was the shore. When it was calm there was a
covering over the water like paint of various hues
shifting and changing, and showing the most singular
sport of this kind that could be imagined. There
were great herds of cattle feeding in the swamps in
winter and ranging in the grasses of the pine woods
during the summer. These pines gave them a home-
like feeling for they had seen none in the whole two
thousand miles of their travels on the "Nile of the
West." Mr. Flint was interested in the relics of the
long history of the Floridas, and in the contrasts of
soil, climate, and people compared with other sections
in which he had lived. The shipping on the bayous
and lakes he found very important, but the sailors were
the most abandoned of their class, being the refuse
from the sea and larger rivers. The native people he
thought were more shiftless and degraded than in other places, being generally denominated Bogues and
calling themselves "rosin heels." [260]

Mr. Flint had charge of two churches here, the one
in Madisonville on the north shore of the lake, a
summer resort for New Orleans people, and the other
at Covington. This latter place was six miles inland,
the county town in St. Tammany County, and the head
of river navigation toward the Mississippi Territory.
There was a school here which Mr. Flint conducted
in addition to his duties as a minister. Only two
things which seemed worthy of note occurred in his

[260] Flint. *Recollections*, 315-319.

work here.   Contrary to the rule in this section, the people were united, and punctual in their attendance on religious worship.[261]   Another occurrence in the time of their residence here was a severe storm, long remembered, in the fall of 1823.   Mr. Flint compares it with a great storm in New England, in the fall of 1815, just as he was leaving the Atlantic section, and thinks the latter was the more severe.[262]

Health seems to have been good in West Florida, but they returned to New Orleans after seven or eight months in the fall of 1823, thinking possibly to locate permanently in that city.   This question was a matter of "painful solicitude."   Many friends assured them that they were now well enough acclimated to make it safe for them to stay in the city through the summer. Fear of the consequence of such an attempt, and the probability that they would be compelled to leave every summer, decided them, when the opportunity came, to go to Alexandria in the same state.[263]   Nothing is said of returning to the north.   They seemed to be here to stay.   The great business prosperity of the country had made it possible for the family to become independent and comfortable in a short time. The country had many attractions, while the need for the teacher and preacher was great.

Before going to the Red River country, with them, it would be well to look at New Orleans as it was in Mr. Flint's time, not so much for the sake of acquaintance with the old city, but because it will be an aid

---

[261] Flint. *Recollections*, 318.
[262] *Western Monthly Review*, vol. iii, 634.
[263] Flint. *Recollections*, 219, 220.

in the study of Timothy Flint to have followed him
here in his meditations and observations.

Viewed on a bright January morning, New
Orleans had a unique and fantastic appearance, more
like European cities than any other in the United
States, he was told. There was a large and handsome
brick Presbyterian church building and a good society, which had had "the brilliant and pious Larned" [264]
as pastor, and now had a very able man. There was a
large and well conducted hospital, a cathedral and a
female orphan asylum. Concerning this latter insti-
tution, Mr. Flint remarks that the inmates attended
first the Presbyterian and then the Catholic church
and that it was founded by a Mr. Poydras, a man
unique in that time and section for his charities. [265]
This was probably Mr. Flint's first experience in a
cathedral-like building and he seems to have spent
many hours within its quiet walls. It stood in the
midst of the city's noise but its walls were so thick that
all was quiet within. The dead buried beneath the
pavement, the figures of the saints, the dim light, the
unalterable repose and perpetual tranquillity of the
place, made it a haven and a benediction to Mr. Flint.
He could not but compare it with the brilliant, highly
finished and strongly lighted interiors of the Protestant churches, to the disadvantage of the latter. [266]

[264] Flint. *Recollections*, 302-304. About Larned, 69, 350.

Reverend Sylvester Larned, born at Pittsfield, Mass., Aug. 31, 1796,
graduated at Middlebury College, 1813. He studied theology at Princeton
and was ordained to the Presbyterian ministry in 1817. He went out as a
missionary in 1817 to New Orleans. He was distinguished as an eloquent
and powerful preacher. He died of yellow fever in New Orleans, Aug. 31,
1820. See *Life and Eloquence of the Rev. S. Larned*, by R. R. Gurley.

[265] Flint. *Recollections*, 305, 306.

[266] — *Idem*, 304.

Mr. Flint took careful note of the moral conditions of the city. He did not believe, as was generally reported, that it was worse than other large cities of the country. There was a very efficient police system and there was no complaint of the law's delays. There were certain sections of the city and certain houses so bad and having such an aspect of "beastliness and degradation, as to render them utterly *unbearable*." But Mr. Flint thought it was possible that these places rendered the same service to the city as the "Helotes, to the Spartan children." There was more of a babel of tongues here than anywhere else, and as seen and heard in the market place it was an experience not to be forgotten. The French were the same gay and light people everywhere. Their great, brilliant, and gaudy theater was crowded on Sundays. But as indication that not all the people of the city had the same mind about Sunday amusements, Mr. Flint tells us that he noticed, one Sunday morning, large theater bills posted about the city, announcing the play for that evening. He says:

> Towards evening of the same Sabbath I observed that a paper of the same dimensions, and the same type, but in English, was everywhere posted directly under the French bill. It contained appropriate texts from the Scriptures, and was headed with these words; "Remember the Sabbath day to keep it holy," and mentioning that there would be divine service at a place that was named, in the evening.[267]

There were many societies and unions whose mission it was to pour salt into the city's fountains. There was "apparently much excitement of religious feeling." During the second winter of his residence, Mr.

[267] Flint. *Recollections*, 307, 309.

Flint took an active part in a lecture course which was
conducted by the ministers of the city.[268]

Next to the vice of the city the saddest side of its life,
to Mr. Flint, was the awful sickness and mortality.
The hearse was busy night and day.   In the summer
of 1822 the destroying angel had seemed to carry a
"besom" and there were two thousand recorded deaths
beside multitudes unnoted.   The poor Catholic-Irish
and the northern young men suffered most.   The latter, he thought, had but one chance in two of surviving
the first fever season.[269]

Sin and sickness filled the cemeteries.   Part of the
dread of burial there, came from the fact that for a
large part of the year the water filled all graves that
were not built above ground.   The Catholic cemetery
was full of graves and monuments, one wall being
formed by contiguous monuments in two tiers.   It
was here that Mr. Flint delighted to wander on moonlight evenings, meditating on the transient dream of
life, and the vanity of the search for wealth which
brought so many from every clime, to end their days
in this place.[270]

Two inscriptions in this cemetery were impressed
upon his memory.   One was on a handsome slab in
the upper tier, and in gilt letters, *Il moruit victime
d'honneur.*   From this pitiable eulogy of the duel he
turned with pleasure to a simple stone erected by a
master for his black servant, with its eulogy of the
long, faithful, and affectionate service of the slave.
He turns from these cities "of the living" telling us
that in the Protestant cemetery he had seen, a great

268 Flint. *Recollections*, 311, 319.   269 — *Idem*, 311.   270 — *Idem*, 312.

number of the names of young men from Salem, Boston, and all New England, who had died in the prime of their life "du fievre jaune." [271]

Mr. Flint had a keen appreciation of the great commercial advantages of New Orleans. He thought its location was unrivaled by any other city in the world and that it far surpassed New York in this respect. With a clergyman from the north he estimated the number of boats along the river front at between twelve and fifteen hundred. With the unlimited capacity for productiveness in the upper country, the trade of which at that time all came down the river, and the products of all climes finding their way thither by the sea, Mr. Flint could hardly imagine the future of this city. [272]

[271] Flint. *Recollections*, 312, 313.   [272] — *Idem*, 301, 308.

X. THE HOME ON THE RED RIVER

Not New England, but Louisiana, was to become the home of Timothy Flint's family. At Alexandria, on the Red River, some two hundred miles above New Orleans, this family took deep root, even before the death of its head in 1840. All connection with the land of its birth was lost after a few years and it became an integral part of the Southland. There many of its members are found today.

Not far from the beginning of the year 1824, the removal took place and under conditions far more comfortable than any of the previous travels of this family. The steamer Spartan was chartered to carry them and a few other passengers. They made a speedy and delightful trip to their new home.[273]

The waters of the Red River were not unlike those of the Arkansas and deserved their name. The channel was in most places narrow and deep, though very sinuous. Shoals of alligators were seen crossing the stream, "as though logs had found the power of locomotion." Alexandria was found to be a pleasant village, one hundred and fifty miles by river, above the Mississippi, though but one third that distance in a right line. It was on a perfectly smooth plain, carpeted with the richest verdure, which sank away into the cypress swamps a few miles back from the river.

[273] Flint. *Recollections*, 320, 321.

On the opposite and eastern bank of the river, the pine
bluffs came near. The white houses with their piazzas,
showed themselves under the beautiful china and ca-
talpa trees. The music of the falls just above the
village, reminded them of the distant roar of the Atlantic, and lulled them pleasantly to sleep.[274]

Alexandria was in the center of one of the most
important cotton districts of the south. It was the
seat of justice for the parish of Rapide. There were
bankers, lawyers, doctors, and editors enough but the
country was new and the state of literary culture was
very low. The college, over which Mr. Flint pre-
sided, was in a huge but rather ugly building. It had
absorbed great sums of money, and was still supported
generously by the state and by its patrons. There
were large numbers of students, many of them board-
ing with the principal. The work was elementary
but none the less laborious. Three Presbyterian ministers had already laid their ashes here, one of them
the Reverend Mr. Hull having died just before Mr.
Flint took charge of the seminary and church.[275]

Mr. Flint found his work very pleasant but exact-
ing for a man of such limited strength as his. The
preaching demanded was of the highly emotional type.
He was very much isolated as to fellowship, the nearest
minister with whom he could exchange being at
Natchez, two hundred and fifty miles distant by river.
The roads were much nearer but impassable most of
the year. There were only three Baptist churches in
the state, and Mr. Flint's church was the only one of
its order in that part of the state. The Methodists

---

[274] Flint. *Recollections*, 322, 323.   [275] — *Idem*, 323.

were at work with their usual zeal; but their hostility to slavery limited them very much in their immediate sphere of influence. There were many Catholic churches. The religious and social conditions seemed hopeful to Mr. Flint, there being some things that he would like to have seen transferred to the more serious people of the north.[276]

Mr. Flint says the first year in Alexandria passed very pleasantly "in the discharge of uniform duties." His society was small but embraced some of the most amiable families that he had anywhere met. The people were very attentive to his ministry.[277]

It was here that Mr. Flint met Judge Henry Bullard, who became one of his most intimate and valued friends. We have already noticed that the father of this man, Reverend John Bullard of Fitchburg, Massachusetts, was a neighbor and friend of Mr. Flint, when he was at Lunenburg. The judge was eight years younger than Mr. Flint, but he was a Harvard man, 1807, and in every way congenial.[278] Mr. Flint says about him in the *Recollections*:[279]

> If any one would know the value of a companion, bred in the same region, formed to similar habits, versed in all kinds of literature, a scholar, a gentleman, and a man capable of sincere and ardent friendship, let him wander without such a friend ten years in the wilderness of the West, and then, where such a thing was least expected, let him find such a friend.

In the preface to *Francis Berrian*, Mr. Flint pays a warm tribute to the friendship of Bullard. He also

---

[276] Flint. *Recollections*, 340, 341.

[277] — *Idem*, 353.

[278] See Harvard *Class Book for the Class of 1807*, in Harvard Library, manuscripts department.

[279] Page 353.

says that this story grew out of conversations with the judge and that he is indebted to him for much of the material in it: "You well know, that no inconsiderable portion of these adventures is anything, rather than fiction." [280]   Judge Bullard had spent several years in Mexico as a soldier of fortune, before he settled at Alexandria.   Much of the interest of *Francis Berrian* comes from this mingling of the story of his friend with the writer's fiction.

In the village of Alexandria, clean and delightful every way to the eye, they had a comfortable residence near the school building.   The breezes were pleasant, but in them, carried from the wide spreading swamps, were the deadly fever germs.   Here, as every where in this section, Mr. Flint says, the rich soils were the places of greatest danger, and the poor soils of the pine woods the healthiest.   Late in May, 1824, Mr. Flint being quite ill at the time, the family retired to the pine woods where they built a cottage near those of two other families with whom they were intimate, Judge Bullard's family being one of them doubtless. Here in the woods there was a considerable settlement of people from Alexandria and the region about. [281]

This summer in the pine woods is the pleasantest and most idyllic of any that we have recorded in Mr. Flint's life.   And so he thinks himself. [282]   There was every charm of nature, charms to which he and his family were most responsive.   There was also the rare blessing of health and vigor.   He was seized by a "poetical paroxysm," and wrote:

---

[280] Flint. *Francis Berrian*, p. iii.
[281] Flint. *Recollections*, 353-364.
[282] — *Idem*, 355.

> For I remember well the scorching day,
> When weary, faint, and wan, I saw thee first,
> Expecting soon to lay the load of life
> Beneath the turf; but thy cool wave
> And healthful breeze inspired other hopes.[283]

They were in comfort, and in the midst of warm and cherished friends. The keenness of their pleasure is perhaps best indicated by the poems written at this time, which recite their experiences and meditations.[284]

Continuing his song of the forest and stream, Mr. Flint says:

> Thy fountains, springing midst the wavy pines,
> Well from the hills, to join thee, o'er a sand
> As pure as mountain-snow; so bright,
> That the gay red-bird tunes his note of joy,
> Soon as he settles on thy laurel branch.
> How often, ere the jocund morn had ting'd
> Thy groves with gold, my angling rod in hand,
> From thy pellucid wave I've drawn the trout,
> In all his pride of mottled white and gold,
> And born the cumbrous prize, triumphant, home.

There was no "jealous lock or latch" in their Eden, for:

> By joint consent with these dear friends we threw
> Observance, form and state all to the winds.

Three or four families took many of their meals together. The breakfasts were eaten under the beaches near the stream where the abundant trout—Mr. Flint caught over two thousand of them averaging over a

---

[283] Flint. *Recollections*, 356.

[284] Beside the two poems written at this time by Mr. Flint and Micah, there is a third poem written by the latter at some other time which is closely related to this occasion and experience. Mr. Flint incorporates it here with this summer's experiences. See *Recollections*, 359-364.

pound in weight, during this summer – were tossed by
the anglers to the black girls who did the cooking.

> And then, when evening from the azure east,
> Threw her deep mantle o'er the dark-brown pine,
> We've sat, well pleased, to list the breezy moan,
> Nature's Eolian harp, to sink, or swell
> Along the boundless forest-tops, in strains,
> That awe, impress, or council sleep: –
> This vesper hymn prolong'd, till the bright moon,
> Thron'd on her silver car, and twinkling stars
> Seem but to float just o'er the forest tops.
> Sudden the blazing torches rise around,
> And pour their flickering light amidst the trees,
> And spread illusions o'er our humble sheds,
> As those, that mark enchantment's fabled tales.
> Our cabins turn to palaces, and the dark pine,
> Seen half in living light, and half in shade,
> Half lucid verdure, and half deepening gloom,
> Shows, like the light of life, shut by the grave
> From the dark regions of eternity.[285]

As Mr. Flint looked back on these happy months
he could detect that even then there was a "sad pre-
sentiment" hanging over him.   He seemed always to
fear when the cup of happiness was at his lips lest it
betoken a bitter one to follow.   Micah's lines written on this same occasion would be expressive of the
father's feelings.   Micah says:

> And, lost in thought, how deeply pondered,
> On my distant native land.
>
> .   .   .   .   .
>
> Her granite cliffs, that breast the ocean,
> Dashing back the Atlantic wave.

How soon and how sadly the father was to see those

---

[285] Flint. *Recollections*, 356, 357.

granite shores, neither of them could know, when they
went back to the village in the fall, singing:

> Farewell, ye groves, that I am leaving,
> Where I've spent the summer heats;
> Autumnal gales now force us, grieving,
> To resume our winter seats.[286]

The *Recollections*,[287] tell the story of the few months
that followed the return from the hills. A part of
it is as follows:

> In October of the last year, we resumed our laborious duties
> in the Seminary. I had my son and another young man under
> a particular course of personal instruction. I had boarders, a
> numerous school, preached after a sort and as I could, and was
> trying to digest this work. A few weeks of this overplied exer-
> tion began to make me feel the illness, which brought me to your
> country. I struggled to vanquish it, by resolution and exercise,
> until the eighth of last December. I was then seized with a
> bilious complaint, accompanied with spasm, which confined me to
> my bed. All the aids of medicine were unavailing. The middle
> of January, I was just able with assistance, to mount on horse-
> back. Accompanied by my friend, Judge Bullard, of whom you
> have so often heard me speak, I commenced a journey to Natchi-
> toches and the interior beyond for my health.

There is a full description of this journey to and
from the Mexican frontier on the Sabine River. But
we must confine ourselves to the things that most intimately concern Mr. Flint.

They journeyed slowly and at first the sick man
gained some strength. Their coming was known and
everywhere the planters vied with each other in their
attentions to the minister and judge. At Natchitoches,
they spent two weeks, most hospitably entertained,
and were deeply interested in the old town. Mr.

---

[286] Flint. *Recollections*, 357, 358.   [287] — *Idem*, 364 ff.

Flint speaks of its history as a succession of Indian *powwows*, Spanish *fandangoes*, French balls and American frolics.   To tell the story he must be the "great Unknown," and "have ten volumes for elbow." "Pity, that all this interesting matter should be lost, for want of an historian," says Mr. Flint.[288]

He was called upon here to act as chaplain for a French surgeon named Prevot, who was to be hanged for killing a young attorney from the north, a Mr. Mills, because he would not fight a duel with him. The Frenchman belonged to "the school of Voltaire and Delambert," which he said was a bad kind of school to make a good Christian.   He at first refused to talk with Mr. Flint thinking he was a Roman priest. Learning that Flint was a Protestant he said eagerly, "vous avez raison donc."   Mr. Flint accompanied him to the gallows, offered a prayer at the request of the condemned man, saying for him in English to the assembled people, that he died asking the mercy of God, and in charity with all men.   His last words to Mr. Flint were: "Adieu, ministre! je vous remercie."[289]

Mr. Flint and his friend passed on to the Spanish frontier and the village of Adayes.*   This was a typical Spanish village, and the buildings and people offered an interesting contrast to the French settlements. Returning from this point they were lost in the woods for a time and caught in a rain storm before they were finally guided on their way to the United States Post, "Cantonment Jessup."   Here they were welcomed by Colonel Many who commanded two companies of

---

288 Flint. *Recollections*, 366.   289 — *Idem*, 367-369.   * Now spelled Naies.

soldiers.   On reaching Natchitoches again, Mr. Flint
was unable to ride, and returned to his home by boat,
having had little benefit from his excursion.[290]

The illness continued.   During the sultry weather
of March he grew so much worse that friends and physicians joined in urging him to go to the north as a last
resort.   Many cases were cited to him to prove the
efficacy of such a step.   But to the exhausted invalid,

> Who had been for years sustained by the most assiduous nurs-
> ing and care, it seemed a formidable experiment to commit myself
> to such a great journey, and to separate myself from every friend.
>
> .   .   .   .
>
> You know enough of my habits to be aware how often, in my
> days of distress and my nights of watching, I laid my case before
> Him, who alone can help; how often, in the vibrations of feeling,
> different determinations would alternately have the mastery. . .
> A carriage, a horse, a servant, all the little delicacies so
> necessary to the fastidious appetite of an invalid, were constantly
> furnished me by my friends.   Kindness of every sort may be
> rendered, and the heart may swell with grateful thoughts, which
> cannot clothe themselves in words, and yet disease go steadily on.
> So it was with me.   I saw that I could not long survive in that
> region.   I determined to disengage myself from my family, cast
> myself on the care of God, and commence a journey of twenty-five
> hundred miles for my native land, looking forward as the most
> fortunate consummation, that I had a right to hope, to revisit the
> scenes and the friends of my first years, and after so much wander-
> ing and toil, to be buried by the "graves of my father and my
> mother." [291]

So the journey was undertaken on the fourth of
April, 1825.   When he arrived at the home of his
friend, Dr. James Flint in Salem, he said he "had
come home to die." [292]

---

[290] Flint. *Recollections*, 369-373.   [291] — *Idem*, 373, 374.
[292] *Encyclopedia Americana: Supplementary Volume*, vol. xiv, 270, 271.

XI. A NEW LEASE OF LIFE

Mr. Flint in telling the story of this long and painful journey says:

It is unnecessary for me to speak of the forced cheerfulness of my family and my friends, the presages of people, who talked with confidence in their words to me, and who instantly used a different language among themselves. Friendship and kindness could do nothing for me, that was not done. A kind neighbor was to accompany me as far as Baltimore. The morning sun shone brightly. The bell had struck for calling together the pupils in the seminary. They bade me farewell in the court-yard. My family accompanied me to the steps. Perhaps the hardest parting of the whole was with a little fellow between three and four, with a dark Spanish countenance, but a brilliant eye, that easily kindles with joy or is suffused with a tear, according to the passing emotion. He is our Joseph [James Timothy], born to us after an interval of fourteen years, excepting the infant which we lost on the Mississippi. He was marching in the court-yard with his military hat and feather, clad in a new suit, and with a tin sword, given to keep him away from this painful business of parting. But he had come, and saw that there was restrained emotion and uncommon countenances. He came up to me and asked why mama and sister looked so strange. I kissed him, not daring even to turn back, or cast one "longing, lingering look behind;" and sustained by my two sons went on board the steamboat Natchitoches, bound for Natchez, parted from my sons, took my berth, heard the parting gun fired on the bow, and instantly felt, that we were descending the river.[293]

At Natchez two physicians visited and aided him

---

[293] Flint. *Recollections,* 374, ff.

with counsel and medicines.　He took the fine new steamer Grecian for Louisville and made a speedy journey in beautiful weather which he would have greatly enjoyed but for his extreme illness.　There were such mornings as would almost create a "soul beneath the ribs of death."　But all the beauty, and the busy and joyous life on the gay steamer, struck a key not at all in unison with his feelings. Many nights he took a mental leave of family and world, thinking it unlikely that he would survive until morning.　On the eleventh of April he records, "we passed the place where our babe lies buried."　In ten days he had reached Louisville.　What a contrast with their sad and lonely journey up the great river in 1819.　He now traveled one "hundred miles a day, against the whole weight of the Mississippi current."　Then for fifty days they had struggled with the current, and thought ten miles a day good progress.[294]

Louisville had grown to be a fine town, the very smell at the landing indicating a great and growing place.　The log farm houses along the river had given place to houses of brick.　At Cincinnati, he was still more surprised with the change that ten years, or a little less time, had wrought.　He stayed here two days, visited by friends and relatives, and aided by the then famous Dr. Drake.[295]

On the passage to Wheeling his complaint took a new form which still more weakened him, but the striking changes in the country continued to attract

[294] Flint. *Recollections*, 377.　Also *Geography and History*, vol. i, 238.

[295] Mr. Flint speaks of Dr. D., one of the respectable physicians of the place.　He was probably referring to Dr. Drake, a famous physician of Cincinnati and a man that later Mr. Flint was to know intimately.

his notice. He was reminded of Cæsar's changing Rome from brick to marble when he saw the Ohio villages. Wheeling, when he first saw it, "was a smoky, mis-shapen village." Now he found rows of massive brick buildings, and lodged in a hotel equal to anything on the Atlantic coast. The great national road from here to Baltimore seemed even more marvelous than other changes and especially as he remembered their first toilsome and dangerous journey to Pittsburg over the mountain road. The land travel was more exhausting than the river. At Washington, Pennsylvania, he was obliged to rest two days, receiving much kindness and attention, but being still further inconvenienced for traveling in a stage, by the application of a large blister.[296]

Speaking of the journey through the mountain region, Mr. Flint says:

We were driven down the most considerable of them, a distance of between four and five miles, at a furious rate, and at midnight, and just on the verge of precipices, that it would be fearful to look down upon at mid-day. I suffered more than I can describe, from weakness and exhaustion. We crossed the Potomac, stayed a night at Frederick, and I was cheered with a distant view of the Atlantic regions. . . Having arrived in Boston and met some friends, who are very dear to me, and from whom I parted between ten and eleven years before, as I departed for the West, I could see by the very attempt to suppress surprise and exclamation, how time and disease had changed my countenance. . . A few hours brought me to you, my dear friend [Dr. James Flint, Salem], and having accomplished the object of my prayers, having seen again my earliest and most constant friend, I felt in that joyful hour of meeting, as though, could I have had my family with me, miserable as my health was, I should have

[296] Flint. *Recollections*, 378-380.

been the happiest of the happy. But at the end of this long pilgrimage, with more than two thousand miles interposed between me and my family, your countenance, and that of my other friends, told me but too plainly, that these halcyon hours were not expected to be long repeated. There are no constant things here, but disappointments and tears. Happy for us, that there remaineth a rest for the people of God.[297]

While the father is thus thinking and writing of his family, busy about their home and school duties in the far south, the eldest son is writing:

> . . . I implore his blessing
>   On an absent father's head,
> That, health and hope possessing,
>   He may yet return to spread
> A smile of joy and gladness
>   O'er an anxious mother's brow,
> And chase the look of sadness,
>   Which is there imprinted now.[298]

Here ends not only the story of the long journey home but the *Recollections*. Thus far it was written during the summer in New England, and dedicated at Salem in September to Doctor Flint. At the request of his friend, another letter was written from Cincinnati in September on his way home. This is printed as a supplemental letter in that same volume. In this he gives his impressions of things in New England as he saw them after ten years absence. The very marked industrial, social, and religious revolution, then taking place, was a matter of the greatest interest and concern to Mr. Flint, and he returns to it often in the letters written during the next ten years, in which period he was several times in New England. These

297 Flint. *Recollections*, 380-382.
298 Flint, Micah P. *The Hunter and Other Poems*, 129.

fully recorded impressions are of importance for an understanding of Mr. Flint's character and will be noticed later.

Dr. James Flint says in his article in the *Encyclopedia Americana* that the effect of the climate, of quiet and rest, and of a trip they took together to Saratoga, was to so far restore his friend's health, that he was able to write the *Recollections*.[299] This Mr. Flint did at the urgent request of his friends. This book it appears was all written in New England at this time except the supplement as above noted. The first letter or chapter is dated Alexandria, Red River, October, 1824. Part of this may be a letter written at that date to Doctor Flint, but at least a part of even this letter was written after his return to New England. It is quite possible that he used some of his own letters to Doctor Flint and notes made earlier, but it is to be remembered that he says he wrote "without books" or journal.[300]

Besides the journeys mentioned by Doctor Flint, Timothy probably visited his home in Reading, though he does not mention this visit and seems to have made his head-quarters in Salem. At the home church he found a new minister in the place of the aged Eliab Stone, who had died in August, 1822. His father was still living at the place of his birth and at the advanced age of eighty-eight years. His mother had been dead near twenty years. He revisited Lunenburg where he was greeted as one come back from

---

[299] *Encyclopedia Americana: Supplementary Volume*, vol. xiv, 270, 271. Griswold in his *Prose Writers of America* [152] says that Flint began to write the *Recollections* soon after his removal to Alexandria.
[300] Flint. *Recollections*, 4, 296.

the grave. They had thought of him too, in their
humble annals, as a personage of history. He says
of this experience:

All that ought to have been remembered by my former people
in my favour, was remembered. All that in those days of inex-
perience, of untamed youth and temperament, related to me,
which I could have wished forgotten, seemed to have been completely consigned to oblivion. . . One burst of affectionate
remembrance was manifested by the whole people. I felt painfully, that in wandering from that rustic, but feeling people, I had
wandered from home. This excitement, so many recollections,
alternately delightful and painful, stories of the living, the suffering, and the dead, the necessity of conversing with so many,
soon renewed my indisposition, and I was compelled to hasten
away.[301]

Much restored in health Mr. Flint began in September, the journey to his home in Alexandria. He
had finished his *Recollections* and left the manuscript
with the publishers who brought it out in March of
the following year. Dr. James Flint says that he
began the writing of *Francis Berrian* on the return
trip home, and finished it during the following winter.[302] This story opens with a description of the
writer's journey from Massachusetts to the regions of
the Spanish frontier. Just what is fact and what is
fiction can not be told, as the journey progresses, but
we are enabled to see Mr. Flint making a comfortable
and glad return to his family, enjoying himself with
newly made and old friends on the palatial steamboats, and devoting himself to reading and writing as

---

301 Flint. *Recollections*, 388.

302 Doctor Flint says that *Francis Berrian* was begun on the return journey
in the fall of 1826. As the work was brought out in the summer of 1826, it is
clear that he should have said the fall of 1825. See article in *Encyclopedia
Americana: Supplementary Volume.*

steam and current carried him south. We have also a glimpse of the glad home coming in the *Francis Berrian*.

We do not know whether Mr. Flint resumed his school work or not. His son Micah must have been in the practise of his profession as a lawyer about this time and was perhaps already interested in a plantation. The family circumstances continued to grow easier from the beginning of their residence here. It seems rather likely that Mr. Flint devoted himself chiefly to literary work during the winters of 1825-1826 and 1826-1827. A number of articles that appear in the first numbers of the *Western Monthly Review*, beginning in May, 1827, appear to have been written in Louisiana, and it would seem likely that nearly all of the work on the *Geography and History* was done before he moved to Cincinnati.[303]

On April 27, 1826, Mr. Flint again left his home in Louisiana for an expected absence of eight months. He was ill at the time and this trip was probably taken partly for the same purpose as the one a year before. But he was not nearly so helpless, and hopeless as then, and seems to have had certain business enterprises in mind. Dr. James Flint says he brought the manuscript of *Francis Berrian* with him on this journey.[304] It was published during this summer and while Mr. Flint was in the north. We do not know whether he remained as long as he intended and are only told by Dr. James Flint that he once more rejoined his fam-

---

[303] The *Geography and History* was copyrighted, Oct. 19, 1827. See also the preface to the different editions. See *Review*, vol. i, 69, 71, 81, opposite 310.

[304] See footnote 302.

ily in the autumn of 1826. Some of his time while
in the north must have been spent in literary work,
especially on the *Geography and History* which was
ready for the public in the fall of the next year. He
had these volumes printed in Cincinnati, and it is likely that so extensive a work would take a Cincinnati
printer many months to accomplish. In all probability he completed his arrangements while north in 1826
for removal to Cincinnati and for the beginning of
his magazine and publishing business early in 1827.

In the October number of the first volume of the
Western Monthly Review we have a ten page article
entitled, "Extracts from the Journal of a Voyage from
Alexandria, Red River, Louisiana, to New York, by
way of New Orleans and the Gulf of Mexico." There
are no names but there are unfailing signs in this journal that it is Mr. Flint's and that he was then in "the
laudable habit of taking notes during travels" even
if it had become "the bore to the public."[305] Mr.
Flint is always at his best when describing the experiences of a journey. Of the many such accounts which
we have, none are more interesting than this. It is
the story of the second trip to the north and was made
in 1826.

He embarked at New Orleans, May 1, "in the large,
new ship Azelia, Captain Wibray, to sail next day."
He had spent two days in New Orleans, which place
he had not visited for two years. The nights in New
Orleans were made memorable by the immense band
of large bull frogs in the nearby swamp. "The depth,
number, and variety of the cries of these animals unit-

---

[305] *Western Monthly Review*, vol. iii, 270. For the story of the journey
see vol. i, 313-322.

ed the ludicrous and the terrible." The invasion of mosquitoes through a fissure in the netting, created a situation not only "ludicrous" but so "terrible" that a black girl must drive out the enemy and mend the rent before there could be rest.[306]

At evening time a steamboat gripped the Azelia on one side and a French ship bound for Havre on the other side, and carried them off like "a cat lugging her kittens." By morning they are set free on the "illimitable sea." The leave taking of the French and Americans with the friends to be left behind, the contrasts in the expression of emotions, are of keen interest to this observer who seems equally to wonder at the ways of nature and of man. He joins in spirit with the worship conducted by the Roman priests on the French ship, for do not even the black hands on the grimy tug below, uncover and stand in reverence. The first sight of the sea carries him back to the days of his boyhood and the many hours that were spent in the chill and healthful wave of the Atlantic. But from the smooth river current to the sea is a sharp change and in a few minutes all the bilious passengers are sick. Mr. Flint remains on deck as long as he can see land, dreaming of all that has happened on those receding shores.[307]

For two days he is disabled, but on the third there is a dead calm following the brisk north breeze. For three days they lie motionless in the water with the spires of Havana visible from the topmast. They amuse themselves with the sea birds, turtles, and with sinking objects. All of these latter are turned suc-

---

[306] *Western Monthly Review*, vol. i, 315.
[307] —*Idem*, vol. i, 315-317.

cessively into silver, gold, pearl, and diamond as they
sink in the clear, still water.   The captain and sailors
of a Yankee schooner come on board and furnish
amusement for the passengers with their dialect and
"apparent simplicity."   Even Mr. Flint can see them
with the southern eye, but "apparent" proclaims him
as he always claimed to be "a true son of New England." [308]   After the calm, a storm, and even worse
sea-sickness, which has one virtue; causing an indif-
ference to existence which "excludes fear."   But the
grand spectacle rouses him the second day of the storm.
What the poets have not been able to tell him he can
now see and feel for himself, though he has to be laid
on a mattress in the companion-way, to see it. [309]

On Sunday morning, the sixteenth day of the voyage, the beautiful bay and city of New York open before them.   Here they are only planting.   In New
Orleans was green corn and cucumbers.   The verdure
here is not so deep but looks more healthful.   A Jersey steamboat carrying passengers to church in New
York, for it is Sunday morning, takes them in tow.
"At ten we gladly spring on shore, and I once more
tread *optato gremio telluris*." [310]

One other incident occurring in Alexandria in January, 1826 or 1827, is recorded in a letter probably
written to Dr. James Flint.   It is given because it
shows the things which most impressed Mr. Flint, and
because of its inherent interest.   He was taking his
usual morning walk on a marshy forest road – a walk
so dreary that it had become the subject of frequent

[308] Flint. *Recollections*, 390.
[309] *Western Monthly Review*, vol. i, 320, 321.
[310] — *Idem*, 322.

jest among his friends. He gives us one of his most perfect pictures of the morning scenes and sounds. Into this picture, amidst which he walks thinking of the distant friend of his youth, comes the wail of a woman. Coming along the road are a couple of Indian women and two or three children following in the customary Indian file, a cart upon which is a rude cypress coffin. Preceding it is an aged Indian man. Sympathy in the face and words of this tender hearted man, stops the procession. The aged father answers in his broken French: "c'etoit mon seul fils – c'etoit grand et brave. Mais il est parti, et nous partons." He had heard a father's "funeral oration for his son," and he went on his way, the wails of the widow dying in the distance, meditating upon how "death deals his dart, and tears fall; and hearts are as deeply desolated in the wild woods, as when the tenant of a palace falls." [311]

[311] *Western Monthly Review*, 71-73. Extract from a letter.

XII. LITERARY WORK IN CINCINNATI

After twelve years spent in the great west, and in the early part of 1827, Mr. Flint was able to carry out the object which he had more especially in view when he was first planning to go west. This was the plan, of which he wrote to the Missionary Society of Connecticut, to establish, "in some central place a religious publication, like our religious monthly papers; except that it should more particularly vindicate our literature, charities and institutions." [312] The "central place" was Cincinnati. The publication was the *Western Monthly Review*. The object of the *Review*, as set forth in the editor's inaugural address, holds closely to that which was first in mind.

Mr. Flint probably moved to Cincinnati about the time that his *Western Monthly Review* was first issued, May, 1827. [313] Cincinnati was chosen for the new residence because it offered a central location for his business, because there were friends and acquaintances there, and especially because of its cli-

[312] Letter of Timothy Flint, Lunenburg, July 23, 1815.

[313] Mr. Venable in his *Beginnings of Literary Culture in the Ohio Valley* [348] says the family joined Mr. Flint in the fall of 1825. This is a mistake that might have been avoided by a more careful reading of the *Review*. On the other hand, Doctor Flint in the *Americana* article says Flint did not move to Cincinnati until the fall of 1828. This is too late by a year and a half. Mr. Flint declares in his opening article, *Review*, May, 1827, that for himself and his children his first ties and duties are in Cincinnati. E. H. Flint had opened his book store in that city as early as June, 1827.

matic advantages, being somewhat mid-way between
the north and the south.

The family circumstances must have been quite
comfortable by this time.   We hear nothing more of
private schools and Mr. Flint had ceased to preach
regularly.   Then too, the business enterprises undertaken involved the investment of considerable capital.
In addition to the magazine, a retail book store was
opened, and in connection was a publishing and whole-
sale business.   The second son, E. H. Flint, "Hubbard" the family always called him, was in charge of
the business which was continued as late as 1833, about
the time that Hubbard went south with his father's
family.   The *Review* and many of Mr. Flint's books
were published by his son.   There are also occasional
reprints from his press.[314]

The very cordial reception given by the public to
Mr. Flint's first two books, the *Recollections* and
Francis Berrian, was a strong inducement for him to
venture wholly upon the field of literature.   In his
"Editor's Address" while he is quite sensitive to the
criticisms of his own and his son Micah's books, yet
he is evidently much pleased with the wide reading
which has been given them.

In this inaugural address, Mr. Flint gives several
reasons for establishing such a review as he proposed.

We are physically, and from our peculiar modes of existence,
a scribbling and forth-putting people. . . At the census of
1830 the Mississippi valley will contain more than four millions
of inhabitants. . . Little, as they have dreamed of the fact

[314] Charles Lowell, "Trinitarian Controversy" in *Western Monthly Review*, vol. iii, 109.

in the Atlantic country, we have our thousand orators and poets. We have not a solitary journal expressly constituted to be the echo of public literary opinion. The teeming mind wastes its sweetness on the desert air. The exhausted author, after the pains of parturition, is obliged to drop the dear offspring of his brain into the immense abyss of a public, that has little charity for any bantlings, that do not bring money into their hands, and

> "Where it is gone and how it fares
> Nobody knows and nobody cares."

To foster polite literature in the west, was then the first object named.[315]

This particular object, Mr. Flint felt, was of much importance because, he says: ". . . one, who has not seen can not know, with what a curl of the lip, and crook of the nose an Atlantic reviewer contemplates the idea of a work written west of the Alleghany mountains."

He proposed to be gentle and generous with every aspiring writer. His "function" as well as his motto was, *Benedicere, haud Maledicere.*[316] It seems fair also to say that this was his practice. The only time when he might be fairly charged with breaking over his rule was on some rare occasions when he met the furious sectarian or the fawning politician.

There were enemies, however, against whom he proposed to join forces even with "them of the bloody flag."

> Show us an author who advances an irreligious, or an immoral sentiment, an opinion that has a clear tendency to confound the unchangeable distinctions of right and wrong, unhinge principle, and overturn the social foundations, and we will do our

---

[315] *Western Monthly Review*, vol. i, 9.
[316] — *Idem*, 10, 11, 16.

best to paddle our skiff into the line of battle, and will fight with as hearty good will to the cause, as the best of them.[317]

He had still another object in view. He believed there was very little fairness in the world of reviewers. He thought that for the most part their "censure was malignant," and their praise "nauseous," while their motto was "Lay it on thick. Some will stick." Mr. Flint proposed for himself a new standard in this field.[318]

Besides the magazine, three other works were issued within the first year of the Cincinnati residence. There was first the *Geography and History,* copyrighted in October, 1827, then *George Mason,* and *Arthur Clenning* a few months later. Mr. Flint was now fully launched on his literary career. During the next five or six years, with occasional interruptions from forced journeys to New England in summer and to Louisiana in the winter, usually on account of ill health, this stream of literary productions was continuous. The *Review* never more than paid expenses, and suffered several minor changes in its plans. The first volume has considerable poetry, most of it Micah's. The next volume has less and the last one almost none at all. As the poetry diminished, the translations from the French increased until they occupied a large part of the space in the last numbers. In June, 1830, he announced that the *Review* would be discontinued as then published, and that a quarterly in two annual volumes would be issued. Each volume was to contain at least five hundred pages, and it was to be more scientific than the previous work. The advertisement seemed to leave the future some-

---

[317] *Western Monthly Rev.*, vol. i, 14.   [318] — *Idem*, 16, 17.

what dubious, and dependant upon the response of the public. At any rate we hear no more of the *Western Monthly Review* or any successor to it conducted by Mr. Flint. It might seem that the chief weakness of the *Review* was that it was too ideal and too far in advance of its constituency.

Mr. Flint was engaged in several varieties of literary work. One of his best short stories, "Oolemba" was published in Judge James Hall's *Western Souvenir* for 1829. He wrote several articles for the *Knickerbocker* soon after it began in 1832. These were on Phrenology, Education, and Literature and were published in volume two. He wrote for other magazines and annuals. In 1831 he edited the *Personal Narratives* of James O. Pattie. Pattie was an unfortunate young man who had spent six years wandering in the far southwest, and the Spanish country. He suffered great hardships, left his father, and companions dead in the far country and returned home broken and helpless. Senator Johnson of Louisiana had befriended him, and given him a letter to Mr. Flint when he returned to his home in Kentucky. Flint made it possible for him to publish his adventures, furnishing some material for his book, as well as putting it into shape for the publisher.[319]

One of the earliest and keenest interests of Mr. Flint in the section where he began his literary work, was the experiment of Robert Owen,[320] a remarkable

[319] See R. G. Thwaites's *Early Western Travels*, vol. xviii.

[320] Born at Newton, Montgomeryshire, Scotland, 1771, died 1858. See article in *Dictionary of National Biography* (New York, 1895). Also his *Life* written by himself, 1857, 1858, 2 vols.

For Owen's ideas on socialism and communism, see *Documentary History of American Industrial Society* (Cleveland, 1910), vol. vii, chap. ii.

character who had founded a colony at New Harmony, Indiana. This was a sort of "Brook Farm" community, although it did not have so many cranks in it. The founder kept the control of affairs largely in his own hands, and when things did not go to suit him, or when he grew tired of his hobby, he closed up the business and went back to Scotland.

Owen was a rich manufacturer whose home, when he chose to be limited to one little spot on the earth, was in New Lanark, Scotland. He was a globe trotter of an unusual type for that day. His wealth enabled him to indulge successive hobbies, one of which was the founding of an ideal community. He published pamphlets and used every kind of means to get his visionary scheme before the world. He laid down "twelve fundamental laws, nine conditions of happiness and twenty-eight universal laws," which he thought were all that were necessary to bring in the millenium. He had no use for the Christian or any other revealed religion. Mr. Flint found much to admire about the character of the man, but he had no faith in his social theories and no excuse for his hostility to religion.

In 1828, Mr. Owen challenged the ministry of the country to meet him in debate upon the subject of religion. Reverend Alexander Campbell of Bethany, West Virginia, a leader among the dissenting and liberal elements breaking away from the Calvinistic Presbyterians and Baptists, and founder of the sect which was to become the "Christians" or "Disciples," accepted the challenge. The debate was arranged to take place in Cincinnati, in April, 1829,

one year from date of agreement.   Then Mr. Owen
started on one of his globe trotting trips,[322] visiting his
home, several places in Europe, the West Indies,
Mexico, and the United States, engaged the while in
propagating the gospel of his new social system.   He
was one of those men, Mr. Flint says, who always had
the best of every person he met in argument, at least in
his own mind.   When he left them they were always
counted as converts to the new faith.

Owen arrived in Cincinnati in time for the debate,
with a day or two to spare.   The affair had been
widely advertised, and caused intense interest.   It
continued through eight days.   Mr. Flint sat on the
platform of the Methodist church building where the
debate was held, the much larger Presbyterian building being refused for the purpose, and was enabled to
make a careful study of the people and debaters.
There was so much of human nature evident on this
occasion that Mr. Flint was intensely interested in it.
He gives a very full report of the debate and extensive
reviews of the reports which were published later.
He thought Mr. Owen had winded himself after the
first day, and could do nothing but repeat, each time
his turn came, the platitudes of his system.   Indeed,
Mr. Flint thought that Owen's chief purpose in the
debate was to advertise his social hobby.   Owen was
quick at retort and had somewhat the advantage of
Campbell at this point, but it did not serve to put him
on an equality with his antagonist.

Mr. Flint was greatly interested in what he saw and
heard of Alexander Campbell.   He seemed an inter-

---

[322] For an interesting comment on Owen's travels see *Review*, vol. iii, 145.

esting combination of "Scotch shrewdness and Kentucky hard fight." He was unfavorably impressed with Mr. Campbell's nasal twang, though otherwise he had a good voice, with his many provincialisms and his almost flippant way of using the sacred names. He could not agree with his underlying naturalistic philosophy, and did not like his severely logical way of building up his religious system. But all these were minor matters. Campbell was self possessed, quick of apprehension and at retort—if not the equal of Owen in this respect, he was a skilled controversialist, and had at his command an amazing amount of reading of everything which could bear upon his subject, both ancient and modern.

The liberality of his theological views was the one thing that specially attracted Mr. Flint in this western theologian. He was greatly surprised to find it. His remark is, concerning Campbell's views of Christianity: "They are decidedly of the liberal cast." This discovery, by a man so nearly related to the New England Unitarians, as Mr. Flint was, of a similarity between his own and Mr. Campbell's views, is one indication of a parallelism between New England Unitarians and western "Campbellites" that has received little or no attention from later historians. However it was common at an earlier date, to charge this body with Unitarianism.

Mr. Flint hoped that the result of this debate would be:

> . . . That the empire of bigotry in this quarter will be shaken to its center; that the two extremes of Calvinism and Atheism will be alike rejected by the sober good sense of the people, and that the intellectual pendulum will settle in

its vibrations to the permanent point of reasonable and liberal Christianity.[323]

Mr. Flint's concluding remarks on the Owen-Campbell debate let us into the strained relations between him and the orthodox Calvinists. It was an impossible thing that a rigid Calvinist like Reverend Dr. Joshua L. Wilson, pastor of the First Presbyterian Church in Cincinnati from 1808 until 1846, should have confidence in the theological views of a man like Flint. Doctor Wilson was the man who, a few years later, was to accuse Lyman Beecher – fresh as he was from combating Boston Unitarians – and to bring him to trial for heresy. This too, in Mr. Beecher's own church, the Second Presbyterian Church of Cincinnati.[324]

Soon after Mr. Flint came to Cincinnati, the orthodox party had started a weekly paper called the *Pandect*. Doctor Wilson was one of the editors. In the first number of the paper Mr. Flint's religious position was attacked. The attack would seem to have been very rabid, so much so that Flint did not deign to notice it. Later, December 30, 1828, the same paper made what Mr. Flint called a milder assault, and he replied to it.[325]

One of the charges made against Mr. Flint by the *Pandect* was that "being a professed minister of the gospel" his position was so much the worse. Flint

---

[323] *Western Monthly Review*, vol. ii, 647. On Owen, see *Review*, vol. i, 105-118, ii, 197-201, 639-647, iii, 91-100, 133-145, 427-439. On Alexander Campbell see four of the last named of the above articles and *Review*, vol. ii, 660.

[324] See Henry A. and Kate B. Ford's *History of Cincinnati, Ohio*, 150, 151. See also W. B. Sprague's *Annals of the American Presbyterian Pulpit*, vol. ii, 308-318.

[325] *Western Monthly Review*, vol. ii, 460-462.

held to the early New England idea of the ministry—that a minister was only such so long as he continued to perform the office for which he was ordained.

> The claim of any peculiar and inherent rights and dignities,
> of being once a minister and always a minister, are at least as
> contrary to scripture, reason and common sense, as they are to the
> whole spirit of our institutions.   Piety is a real thing; but the red
> stockings of a cardinal can be put on or off.[326]

When he began his literary work he had been careful to say that he only left the sacred office because he
had long been unable to fulfill its duties, and that he
would rather be accused of any other motive than lack
of reverence for the holy calling, as the cause of his
leaving it.[327]   So far did Mr. Flint go in this notion
of his being no longer a minister, that he even flattered
himself that he did not look like a minister, and he
certainly did not affect the clerical dress.[328]

Mr. Flint will not be behind the editors of the
Pandect in reverence for the Scriptures, though he
can not interpret them as they do.   He thinks, that to
take a naked proposition from the Bible, and make it
stand as a simple categorical assertion, is a method
which makes "a horrid jargon of contradictions" of
this "divine and much injured book."   But the main
point of the charge against Mr. Flint seems to have
been that he did not accept the orthodox statement
concerning the Trinity.   This he admits, and he gives
some of the reasons for his position.[329]

We are not surprised to learn that Mr. Flint is lead-

---

326 *Western Monthly Review*, vol. ii, 594.
227 — *Idem*, vol. i, 19.
328 — *Idem*, vol. iii, 288, lines 34-37.
329 — *Idem*, vol. ii, 460-462.

ing, a few months after the above incident, in a movement to form the "First Congregational Church" in
Cincinnati. This society held its first meetings in
1829, obtained a charter in 1830, and dedicated a
building the twenty-third of May in that year. Timothy Flint's name heads the list of the signers to the
form of union. In the same list are the names of Abigail Flint and Emeline H. Flint, the wife and
daughter. Mr. Flint wrote a hymn for the dedication
exercises, and his name was placed upon a bronze
metal tablet in the church a few years later together
with those of the founders of the church.[330] In 1860
there were "liberal" and "conservative" wings in this
church, contending in the courts over the property.
It was then developed that, while the church had always been known as a Unitarian church, it had not
been called such at its founding because *one* of the
leaders had objected to the name "Unitarian." I
think we hazard none of the facts in the case when we
say that the "one" was Timothy Flint. To any one
acquainted with the theological disputes and parties
of the day there is much of significance in this position of Mr. Flint. He proposed to establish a church
in Cincinnati such as he believed was like those of the
fathers in New England. He would not admit a sectarian name or creed.[331]

In the summer of 1828, Mr. Flint made a trip to
New England. The experiences of the journey are

[330] Letter of George A. Thayer, Cincinnati, Jan. 4, 1908, reporting several items from the records of the First Congregational Church, Cincinnati,
in the Unitarian Library, Boston.

[331] — *Idem.* Also Ford's *History of Cincinnati*, 164, 165; and *The
Unitarian Church Case — Remarks of R. M. Corwine and the Opinion of
Judge Collins* (Cincinnati, 1860).

fully recorded in a letter to Dr. James Flint, printed
in the *Review*.[332] This journey was begun on the
eleventh of July and he returned in September. He
had three stage companions for a part of the journey
from Wheeling to Baltimore: Mr. Robert Owen; a
rigidly orthodox Scotch lawyer; and a woman devoted to the Episcopal faith. There was "no want of
disputation and logomachy." The lady and the lawyer could not tolerate the infidel and soon left him to
Mr. Flint. Owen thought religion of every kind had
been the enemy of the race. Man, he said, was entirely the victim of circumstances, yet he proposed to
save him by changing these same masterful circumstances. He seemed to be purely materialistic. He
was tolerant and gentlemanly toward those who opposed him, but patronizing. It was this trait that had
so sorely tried the lawyer and their female companion. It does not seem to have concerned Mr. Flint, or
perhaps Owen did not find it expedient to patronize
him. This was a liberty that few ever ventured upon
with him. Flint says their argument had "one feature at least worthy of praise. It was marked neither
with boisterousness nor temper." Flint's conclusion
about Owen upon this occasion is that he was a mild,
humane, and polished gentleman, a man of great natural shrewdness who had seen much, "with eyes keenly attentive to what he had seen." [333]

He entered Washington at night. Like a French
town, it appeared best in the moonlight. He thought
it was an index of the country, a prophecy of what was

[332] *Western Monthly Review*, vol. ii, 193-209, 249-263.
[333] — *Idem*, 197-201.

to be rather than a finished plan.   It was a city of villages, cow pastures, and corn fields.   It was more favorable than the sights and sounds of a city, as a place in which the greenhorn Solomons from the country might expand their thoughts, ripen their conceptions, and bring forth many a sublime invention for the good of the nation.   Mr. Flint judged that there was enough money lost in a single day of extra and worse than useless spouting, than would be sufficient, to make the grounds more in keeping with the country's expectations from the metropolis.   These grounds were very trying to him.   They were unenclosed, covered with blueberry swamps and clumps of bushes, and cut up into yellow clay roads.   Where there might have been grass, it was "gnawed up by the roots by hungry cows." [334]

The morning after his arrival in Washington, he wandered about the buildings, from which the legislators had all departed and where no "contracts of scratch and tickle were making."   The Indian figures in the panels seemed to him copied from the tobacco store tribe rather than "the real forest walkers." The patent office excited curious interest and shrewd comment.   There were some "fifteen hundred or two thousand projects to triumph over gravity and friction, time and space, height and depth, and to make fortunes, by catching dame nature napping in some of her most fixed purposes."   But the head itself, when wound up by desire for money and fame, seemed to Mr. Flint, the "most versatile and rapid engine." [335]

[334] *Western Monthly Review*, vol. ii, 203-206.
[335] — *Idem*, 202-207.

Mr. Flint returned home over a new route, up the
Hudson and by way of the Erie Canal. This was a
ten or twelve day trip at that time. It seemed a very
easy and speedy means of traveling compared with his
first journey west in 1815. The canal seemed to him a
herculean achievement for a country in the dawn of
its career. Many incidents of canalboat travel are
told, as it was then a novel experience. He marveled
at what he saw of growth in such cities as Rochester
and Buffalo, places recently sprung up in the forests,
but already boasting of city ways and comforts.[336]

He arrived at Niagara Falls at half past one at
night. Instead of going to bed as his fellow passengers did, he spent the remainder of the clear moon-lit
night, viewing the falls, a spectacle which it had been
almost the first remembered wish of his heart to see.
He saw it "in a temperament, at a time and under circumstances just such," as he would have chosen. He
does not attempt any extended description of the falls
but refers to that which he had written earlier for the
Geography and History,[337] and before he had seen
them. He had dreamed about the falls so often that
the reality was somewhat disappointing. The interest in following Mr. Flint to the falls, is not in his description of them, but in his unconscious revealing of
himself in this experience which opened for him a
new chapter in the volume of truth, new powers in his
own soul, and a new appreciation of the Eternal. He
says:

He must have been obtuse of brain and of heart who could

[336] *Western Monthly Review*, vol. ii, 250-255.
[337] See vol. ii, 428, 429.

have thus contemplated this spectacle alone in this repose of nature, under the light of the moon, and the blue stars twinkling in the cloudless dome of the firmament, and not have thoughts, which the poverty of language can never clothe in words.

Mr. Flint was not one of the "obtuse of brain and heart," neither did he suffer from a poverty of words, but he is too true an artist to attempt a description of this deep experience of the soul.   He was content to impress the picture on his own memory, so that ever afterwards, "with a little fixedness of attention," he might repaint the magnificent vision for his own contemplation.[338]

On the eighth of August, 1829, Mr. Flint began another journey to New England.   This, like the former is reported in a letter to Dr. James Flint.[339]   On the steamer up the Ohio from Cincinnati, one of his companions was a clergyman who knew Mr. Flint only by reputation.   Neither of them had any interest in the universal amusement, cards, and naturally began to "confabulate."   Mr. Flint says of this "confabulation":

In discussing matters and things in our city, I soon became, as I had foreseen would happen, the theme of his remarks. The uncertainty of the light made me able to command my countenance beyond the fear of betrayal. In a conversation of a good long hour "by the Worcester clock," I had the advantage of my good natured friend, of hearing my posthumous and historical valuation addressed to the conscious and concrete flesh and blood, as though it had been an abstract thing without parts, or passions. Woe is me! May our friends annoint us, while we live, with their most bland and precious oil; for on our cold stone such rencounters teach us we may expect little but the true caustic acid. The

[338] *Western Monthly Review*, vol. ii, 255-260.
[339] — *Idem*, vol. ii, 284-295.

gentleman was a zealous religionist, regarding my views of religion, as heretical; and you may imagine what kind of a portrait I obtained from this patient and protracted sitting. But we of the West, who have seen alligators, felt blisters, and tasted calomel, learn not to make wry faces at swallowing a bitter potion. Nevertheless, when I informed him, that I was the gentleman, whom he had condescended to discuss, I would have preferred, for the moment, to have been the subject, rather than the painter.[340]

In January of 1832, Mr. Flint was compelled by the unusual severity of the winter, and the orders of his physician, to go to the south for his health. One result of this journey is a story, the materials for which he gathered from the conversation and story telling on the boat. The story is, "The First Steamboat on the La Plata; or, the Monogamist."[341]

During his residence in Cincinnati Mr. Flint was honored by the citizens of the city in several ways. One of the considerations shown him was giving to him, together with Reverend Mr. Pierpont, a place in the then locally famous picture of Lafayette's Landing and Reception at Cincinnati, by the French artist Hervieu. Neither Mr. Pierpont nor Mr. Flint had been present upon the occasion of the "Landing" but they were nevertheless placed among the prominent citizens gathered at that time.[342]

It was early in the period of his Cincinnati residence that Mr. Flint received another honor and a recognition of his ability as a historical writer. On October 30, 1828, his name was proposed to the Massachusetts

[340] *Western Monthly Review*, vol. ii, 285.

[341] *Knickerbocker*, vol. ii, 321-340, 433-450. See especially the introduction, 321.

[342] *Western Monthly Review*, vol. iii, 440-447. This picture has been lost.

Historical Society as a corresponding member and he was elected as such January 28, 1829.[343]

The materials for following Mr. Flint in any other of his travels, until the summer of 1833 when he visited New England again, are lacking.   For the last two or three years of the Cincinnati residence, there is very little that relates to the daily affairs of Mr. Flint or of his family.   Several books came from his pen during this time, and indicate that he was able for much work, and quite as busy as during the first half of his six and a half years in the city.

[343] Massachusetts Historical Society, *Proceedings*, first series, vol. i, 416, 418.

XIII. NEW ENGLAND AND NEW YORK

Mr. Flint was absent from New England for ten years at the time he first went west. After 1825, he made a number of visits of which we know, to that section up to the time of his death in 1840. This intimate view of New England, by one so loyal and keen as Mr. Flint, and by one who could see it with other eye than that of the native and the partaker in the passing events, furnishes a suggestive study of a very important period in the history of New England. He saw with great concern, the breaking up of the simple agricultural and village society by industrial changes; the passing of the old orthodoxy, and the rule of the state church and ministry. These things which had been the marked characteristics of New England and peculiarly of Massachusetts, he had known and loved in his youth. He was not a man to hold tenaciously to the past but he looked on the changes and the future with an anxious and solicitous eye, knowing better than most of his contemporaries, what these things meant.

During his first visit, he was struck with the number of large new buildings throughout eastern New England. Connecting them with the asperity and earnestness of the religious investigations then so common, he might have judged he says, that these new buildings were the temples of a new worship. So indeed he found them to be, "the worship of the golden shrine."[344]   He spent much time investigating the city of Lowell and its industrial institutions during the summer of 1833.   In his youth he had known the site of this city as a farmstead.   Now it had come to be the equal of many older places called into existence, along with other rivals of a recent day, by manufacturing interests, in the same way that agriculture had conjured up great cities in the forests of the west. In these new eastern cities, there was more of apparent culture and comfort than in the western cities, but he thought the latter the most wholesome and promising for society.   Hard as he knew the lot of the western emigrant to be, he wished that more people would go to the unoccupied lands of the west.   The one redeeming feature that is well worth while, as he sees this gathering of the youth into the factory centers, is, that they are not far removed from the homes of their youth and the graves of their fathers.[345]

The vast numbers of children and youth of both sexes, reared together in the factories, amidst the incessant and bewildering clatter and whirl of machinery, breathing a heated and "unnatural air . . . of cotton."   With minds unoccupied, and with morbid excitements, all looked most serious; and he wondered if New England could escape the fate of Europe. The blanched faces, slender forms, and taper fingers of the factory girls was one result of the new employment.   He could not but compare unfavorably these young women, as the future wives and mothers, with the older type of womanhood, the plump form, the

[344] Flint. *Recollections*, 383.   [345] *Knickerbocker*, vol. ii, 251-253.

round, ruddy, pretty, but unthinking Saxon face of
the farmer's daughter.   Indeed he could not seem to
find this old type any place either in factory city or
country village, except on the faces of the old clocks.
In lieu of them there were "the insect forms, long and
pale visages, covered with calash bonnets, a race apparently imported from Italy." [346]

The skilled workers in the factories, he remarks
were largely foreigners, and they served to add to the
serious problems which called for the most enlarged
philanthropy and religious zeal.   He firmly believed
that in all these great changes the New England character would not be found wanting or "that the cor-
porate arithmetical intellect, which is said not to be
guided by a soul, would be permitted to count upon
the products of the human tenants of these new
establishments, as though they were a part of the
machinery." [347]

On his first visit Mr. Flint noticed many improve-
ments with which he was much pleased.   There was
an air of nobleness in many of the recent buildings.
Use was being made of that abundant material, stone.
It was a wonder to him that the fathers had not been
as wise as the Germans of Pennsylvania, in their use of
this building material.   The newspapers had improved much.   Fine writing could be found in most
of them and he saw nothing more of "the cumbrous
inanity or the tiresome insipidity, that used to fill the
papers."   Everybody seemed to have caught the
forms of good society.   Hardly a farmer's daughter

[346] Flint. *Recollections*, 384, 386, 387.
[347] *Knickerbocker*, vol. ii, 252.

he says, "who cannot keep up a sustained conversation, in good set phrase, upon any given subject." [348]

During the summer of 1828 the lines "On Revisiting the Churchyard of my Native Place," were written. These were called forth by his musings over the
newly made grave of his father who had died in that
year at the advanced age of ninety-one years. [349]

During his visit to New England in the summer of
1829, Mr. Flint made a very careful examination of
the then famous Siamese twins, and gave a three page
account of them in his *Review*. At this time also he
visited the war ship Columbus in Boston Harbor, admired its plain simplicity in comparison with the
flaunting gaudiness of the New York and Liverpool
packets, and then, as was his wont, fell to moralizing
over a possible meeting of this ship with one of its
kind in hostile combat upon the tempestuous brine.

. . . What a sublime idea of human daring, power, con-
trivance and triumph of art over nature; what an affecting em-
blem of the reckless, mad, and wanton wrath and folly of
nations! [350]

The visit which was made in the early summer of
1833, was extended for some two months and the New
England experiences are more fully recorded than in
any other of his journals and letters. This account
was in a letter written to Dr. James Flint, in September, from the Narrows, Long Island, after he had been

---

[348] Flint. *Recollections*, 385-390.

[349] *Western Monthly Review*, vol. ii, 210, 211. Two and more dates are
given in the parish records of North Reading for the birth and death of Mr.
Flint's father. The published genealogies do not give the date of his death
and thus it is uncertain. In this poem Flint says he was "fourscore years
and ten."

[350] *Western Monthly Review*, vol. ii, 286-289.

appointed to take charge of the *Knickerbocker*.[351]
His health was very poor just at this period. It was
one of the cholera years, and he had several premonitions of that dread disease as he journeyed from Cincinnati via Lake Erie and the canal. As several
times before, so he was compelled now to travel, when
so ill as to be often obliged to rest a few days from his
journey, and to seek aid from the local physicians. As
he left the city which had been his home for several
years, very early in the morning, he felt, he says,
that: "There is nothing like the gloom from travers-
ing a sleeping city." The ravages of the cholera
were everywhere visible as he journeyed north. But
it did not wholly prevent his pleasure in the great im-
provements of the country since last he passed that
way, nor his enjoyment of the fine roads—while they
lasted. When all hands must alight and help lift the
stage out of the hole in the midst of a swamp, he is as
jovial over the mishap as in the days of his misfor-
tunes upon the "Father of Waters." While there are
few travelers who "have traversed the whole extent of
the United States oftener than myself," he says, "perhaps none have had so few accidents to record," or "so
seldom encountered the annoyance of personal rudeness." As always, he finds friends. "General Mil-
ler, late Governor of Missouri," remained with him
during his detention from his journey by sickness.

He objects to the "shelves" on the canal boats (and
even on the elegant steamboats where it was the same),

---

[351] *Knickerbocker*, vol. ii, 242-263. Mr. Gallagher said in the Cincinnati *Mirror*, July 6, 1833, vol. ii, 168, that Mr. Flint had taken charge
of the *Knickerbocker*.

which are so narrow that a sleeper could not turn over, and so short that a man above five feet ten could not stretch himself in them. On this journey Mr. Flint seems to have had his first experience on the railroad. He says of it:

> In passing on the rail-road from Schenectady to Albany, one experiences the unique sensation, with which it must require a long time to become familiar, resulting from the swift motion of a long line of cars following the smoking engine, as if it were a thing of life. The gentleness of the motion renders it difficult to estimate its rapidity, which is easily measured, however, by the apparent dizzying flight of trees and fences.[352]

He spent a month with Doctor Flint and they visited their birth place in North Reading. Here, he says:

> We once more saw together the church where we were baptized, and the church yard containing the remains of our parents and our kindred, the place of our first thoughts and imaginings, and beheld the faces of our kindred, and the companions of our first days, that still survive. What a change had time wrought, since our last visit to the same places!

He visited for the second time, his former parish of Lunenburg, "where," he says, "before I became a sojourner in the distant west, I terminated a ministry of fourteen years." Since then he had wandered so far, experienced so much, and labored in pursuits so far from this place as to cause doubts whether his experiences here were remembrances or dreams. "The whole seemed like the consciousness of transmigration, and of having long been in a different mode of being from that I passed here."[353] About the time of his visit, Lunenburg was in the midst of a very bitter theological controversy which resulted two years later

---

[352] *Knickerbocker*, vol. ii, 250-251. [353] — *Idem*, 251, 253, 254.

in the organization of a Trinitarian church.[354] This latter church, as in so many places proved the most vital, and the old church of which Mr. Flint was pastor ceased to exist as an organization in 1867.[355]

Mr. Flint traveled in New Hampshire and Massachusetts extensively at this time and the saddest thing of all that he saw in this region was two or three churches where formerly there was but one, "erected as hostile spiritual batteries against each other, where the means of the whole place, were with difficulty adequate to the support of a single minister." "We everywhere heard the bickering and tale bearing of mutual efforts at proselytism." The sacred "wedlock" character of the old pastorate was gone.

> Strange that all this should grow out of the inculcation of the religion of the Prince of Peace! . . . The more minute and undefinable the question of dispute, the fiercer and more embittered the quarrel about it, and the more positively eternal salvation is made to depend upon embracing or rejecting it.

But he always sees a bright spot even if it is far removed and somewhat clouded:

> The gas of human pride and intolerance of opinion would be dangerous, if it remained pent up in the human breast. Perhaps it escapes as safely through this valve, as that of politics, or of philosophical dogmas. Unhappily the ultimate tendency is to bring contempt and reproach upon the worthy name, by which we are called.[356]

In Boston he attended a meeting of his class, thirty-three years having elapsed since their graduation. This was the first time he had been able to meet with them in many years. The meeting was held at the

---

[354] See *Congregational Year Book* (Boston, 1909), 238.
[355] Lunenburg *Parish Records*.
[356] *Knickerbocker*, vol. ii, 254.

home of Lemuel Shaw, chief justice of the state. Of this meeting Mr. Flint speaks very feelingly. He says: "and in that long interval the stern king of the scythe and hour glass had scathed our numbers with a deadlier mortality, than the issue of the severest battle." It was a proud roll that they called. "Our heroes and sages, upon our showing, only wanted their Homers and Pindars, to have figured with the best." But most of the number had forever ceased from college trick and quip and crank, as from all life's labors.

> Gray hairs reminded us, the survivors, that we could not be far behind. . . I have not passed an evening calling forth more kindness of feeling. The mirth was of the cast that cheers the heart, indeed, but springs from the same fountains which give birth to tears.[357]

Mr. Flint had located "at the Narrows, on Long Island, in view of the splendid bay of New York, studded and whitened with sails, and in front of the fresh and verdant landscapes of Staten Island," early enough in September to take charge of the October number of the *Knickerbocker*. It does not seem that he ever brought his family to New York, or that he resided here more than a month or two at this time. He was in very poor health when he took charge of the magazine and seems to indicate in his first editorial, that he regarded the step as a doubtful experiment on this account.

The *Knickerbocker* was in its second volume, and it was the fourth number which Mr. Flint edited. It had been without an editor-in-chief for six months, ever since Mr. Charles Fenno Hoffman had retired in March. The acting editor, Samuel Daly Langtree,

---

[357] *Knickerbocker*, vol. ii, 261-263.

had charge in the interim and again after Mr. Flint's departure. Mr. Langtree's statement in the magazine about editorial affairs, indicates that Mr. Flint was in full charge of but the one number, that for October, 1833. Mr. Langtree says:

> During the remainder of the time that distinguished scholar was announced as editor of this periodical, the precarious state of his health did not permit his residing in this city: and his final resignation, from the same cause, made no further derangement in its direction than the withdrawal of his name.[358]

Doctor Flint also says that his cousin retired from the magazine before the end of 1833. However, he supplied much of the material for the magazine until February, 1834. His actual retirement from the magazine must have taken place then, before the end of the year, and he would be at home in Cincinnati until about January of 1834, when he moved back to Alexandria, Louisiana.

Mr. Flint's relations with the proprietors at this time, Messrs. Peabody and Company, and with the editor in charge, Mr. Langtree, were most cordial. He was held in high esteem and honor by them. But the magazine was bitterly attacked by a few enemies of Mr. Flint even before he took charge of it, under the misapprehension that he was already the editor. This misapprehension had probably risen from the fact that he had already contributed leading articles to the magazine after the retirement of Mr. Hoffman. It is possible also that Mr. Flint had some family ties with the Peabody of this firm, as he had with the Salem family of that name.

On taking editorial charge of the *Knickerbocker,*

[358] *Knickerbocker*, vol. iii, 320.

October, 1833, Mr. Flint said that he had some doubts
about the wisdom of his past course of attempting to
overcome abuse by silence, "and to enact saint among
the children of Belial." He meant still to continue
"under the banners of the peace society, but no longer
to the limit of eschewing self-defence." [359] Accordingly he availed himself of this new indulgence in the
October number of the *Knickerbocker*, to even up
with the editor of the *American Monthly Review,* and
with Judge James Hall of Cincinnati. The latter had
sarcastically and wittily ridiculed Flint's "Lectures
upon Natural History" in his *Western Monthly Magazine.*[360] The former had attacked him on account of
the same book in a long review.[361] Both critics of
Mr. Flint had room to criticise this work and the *Review* made some fair criticisms, but they were, as
Flint says, "malignant," if not "lumbering and dull."
Flint proves himself very skillful at newspaper abuse,
but it is the most disappointing piece of work which
his pen has left.[362] The only excuse is that he did
what the majority of his time were doing.

About the time Mr. Flint took charge of the *Knickerbocker*, Mrs. Trollope's *Domestic Manners of the
Americans* was being very widely read and most in-
dignantly commented upon. Mr. Flint's intimate
acquaintance with Mrs. Trollope during her residence
in Cincinnati, covering a period of perhaps a year and
a half, soon after Flint established himself and family
in that city, had led to his being asked he was sure, "a
thousand times, what sort of person was Mrs. Trollope, and what were her objects in visiting America?"

---

[359] *Knickerbocker*, vol. ii, 241.
[360] Vol. i, 262-273.
[361] Vol. iii, 261 ff.
[362] *Knickerbocker*, vol. ii, 310.

He devoted several pages to answering this question
and to a criticism of Mrs. Trollope's book.[363] His
description of her personal appearance, and of her
habits in society, and judgment in business matters is
not very complimentary, especially in view of Mrs.
Trollope's warm expressions of approval of Mr. Flint.
She had said many things complimentary, and put in
a note in her first volume to say: "The pleasant, easy,
unpretending talk on all subjects, which I enjoyed in
Mr. Flint's family was an exception to everything
else I met at Cincinnati." [364] Mr. Flint thinks that her
business ventures could not possibly have succeeded,
and that her judgment of church, state, and society
were absolutely without value. Moreover he thinks
that if she had been wise enough to have secured en-
trance to the best society, as she might have done in
Cincinnati, and if she had used the sixteen or seventeen thousand dollars that she foolishly sunk in business, to open an account at the local bank,
"she would have been dinnered and toasted and the
fashion. . . America would have been an ocean
of milk and honey. The people would have been
lamblike, and half saints. In short she would have
found everything just as far south-west toward para-
dise, as she has now found it north-east *a l'infer.*"[365]
He is complimentary in speaking of her wide reading,
and very extensive acquaintance with noted men and
great events in Europe. There is one thing that he
thinks she knows very well how to do, and that she has
done well in her book. He says: "Manners, when

[363] *Knickerbocker*, vol. ii, 286-292.
[364] Trollope, Mrs. *Domestic Manners of the Americans*, vol. i, 128, note.
[365] *Knickerbocker*, vol. ii, 292.

and where she chooses, she describes well, for it is in her line." This admission by Mr. Flint is significant when we read some of the things that she said about American manners, as she found them at Cincinnati, such as the following:

> My general appellation amongst my neighbors was "the English old woman," but in mentioning each other they constantly employed the term "lady"; and they evidently had pleasure in using it, for I repeatedly observed, that in speaking of a neighbor, instead of saying Mrs. Such-a-one, they described her as "the lady over the way that takes in washing," or as "that there lady, out by the gully, what is making dip-candles." Mr. Trollope was constantly called "the old man," while draymen, butcher's boys, and the laborers on the canal were invariably denominated "them gentlemen." [366]

During her whole stay in the country she says she did not hear a sentence elegantly turned and correctly pronounced from the lips of an American.

> Were Americans, indeed, disposed to assume the plain unpretending deportment of the Switzer in the days of his picturesque simplicity (when, however, he never chewed tobacco), it would be in bad taste to censure him; but this is not the case. Jonathan will be a fine gentleman, but it must be in his own way. Is he not a free-born American? Jonathan, however, must remember, that if he will challenge competition with the old world, the old world will now and then look out to see how he supports his pretensions.[367]

Mr. Flint remarks further about some of these customs that Mrs. Trollope condemns, as for instance "the villanous and filthy and savage and universal habit, growing into use even by boys, of chewing and smoking tobacco." During a recent long journey this habit had forced itself upon his observation and espe-

[366] Trollope, Mrs. *op. cit.*, vol. i, 140.
[367] — *Idem*, 167.

cially since Mrs. Trollope had called his attention to it. It is too true he admits that "Americans are most filthily given to spitting, though they do not, as the Edinburgh [*Review*] says, spit as soon as they are born, and spit through life, and spit out their expiring breath." Mr. Flint is willing that Mrs. Trollope should "apply the lash to these vile customs."

Let her correct the visible rudeness and boorishness of manners, that seems to be growing up from our habits of equality, and being all as though inmates of a public house on the road and in steamboats. Her rebukes have already done visible good. May they still do more. There is ample space for further improvement.[368]

While Mr. Flint's connection with the New York magazine was very brief, yet it is important because it lets us far into his thought and work at this period. Mr. Langtree, the editor of the *Knickerbocker*, takes a very kindly leave of Mr. Flint in the February number of his magazine, as follows:

One thing we are glad of, which is, that the eminent scholar and distinguished man – the Father of the Literature of his Country – whose name lately honored this Magazine, had happily resigned its charge in time to spare his venerable age the mortification of witnessing the unworthy fact, that a character which abroad is reverenced, and respected, and admired, as it should be, could not, at home, avail to prevent the wretched insult and pointless jest which every little scribbler seemed elevated in the consciousness that he was able to discharge.

We care not for the storm: but, illustrious man! for the credit of this country, and for the honor of humanity, we feel rejoiced, that *thou* wilt see no more of that spirit which, however we know that it existed, we had still hitherto supposed would, toward such as thee, have forgotten its acerbidity.[369]

---

[368] *Knickerbocker*, vol. ii, 291.
[369] — *Idem*, vol. iii, 160.

XIV. TRAVELS IN FOREIGN COUNTRIES

When Mr. Flint gave up his work in New York and moved with his family from Cincinnati to Alexandria it might seem that he was ready to live there quietly for the remainder of his days. But it was during the first year or two of this residence in the south, in 1834 and 1835, that his travels became more extended than at any other period in his life. The chief reason for this was the one that had several times before sent him on long journeys – the search for health. Besides this there was now a freedom from business cares and sufficient means for such expenses, not to mention the old love of travel which still remained with him, that caused him to venture into new and widely separated portions of the world.

Mr. Flint speaks of his own reasons for traveling at this period of his life. He says he was like other invalids who were compelled, with the sea-fowl and the swans to "anticipate the autumnal northern storms, and sail before them to the land, 'where the citron tree blooms,' and frost is unknown. . ." [370] More than once before, and now again, he recovered his health, while on some long, and what would be to most invalids, a most trying journey. He seemed to find relief in the very strangeness and novelty of his surroundings. It was not only the change of climate

[370] "Sketches of Travel, Number Two," in *Knickerbocker*, vol. v, 279.

that he sought but "to beguile the time rendered weary by ill health . . . to distract, by noting diversity of character, objects, and incidents, the painful attention, which undiverted, an invalid is too apt to turn in upon the observation of the ever-varying symptoms of his illness." [371] Under these circumstances, he began, after only a few months in Alexandria in the early part of 1834, what was probably his most extended journey. The records, or those which have thus far been discovered, are quite fragmentary, but it seems that he left Alexandria about the first of April and journeyed to the north.

Just before this trip was begun there was a great fire in Alexandria, which occurred upon the evening of the thirtieth of March, 1834. We have Mr. Flint's vivid description of this. He had seen two or three of the most destructive fires that had ever occurred in the history of our cities. But the brilliant young foliage, the deep, calm, red waters of the canallike river, furnished a background which made this "A Splendid Spectacle," though he was not unmindful of the morning, "when the bright sun should have robbed the scene of its enchantment." [372]

The next word from Mr. Flint is in a *Knickerbocker* article, "Sketches of Travels," [373] where he says:

Near the close of May, at the gray of the dawn of a delightful New-England Spring morning, I rolled away from Boston over the Charlestown and Malden bridges, on a tour to – among other places – Lake Winnipisaukee, and the White Mountains of New-Hampshire.

371 *Knickerbocker*, vol. v, 284.
372 — *Idem*, vol. iv, 295, 296.
373 — *Idem*, vol. v, 242-245.

The turf was a carpet of the tenderest and most brilliant verdure. The fruit trees in full blossom, the air rife with a delicious aroma. On the route through Reading, Andover and Haverhill, he communes with himself saying Peace to you, my native New Englanders! He dared not go further in recording his thoughts at this time. The birth place of Harriet Newell in Haverhill was pointed out to him and led him to remark about her memoirs, about the unequalled circulation of the little book, the "true pathos, the deep feeling, the exalted poetry of religious sentiment" which abounded even in the midst of much tiresome repetition.

He had not heard the Merrimac "celebrated for its beauty: but rolling along its green banks, dashing over its rocks, filling its noble channel," it struck him as a singularly romantic and beautiful river. The White Mountains were still white with snow when they "began to stand forth on the Northern horizon, glittering in the beams of the declining sun." They seemed to him "the noblest mountains in North America, east of the Mexican piles of Orizaba." [374]

The traveler dwells briefly upon scenes and places in New Hampshire and sails down Lake Champlain and passes it with a single, "charming," leaving its further description to other travelers. On the shores of Canada he pauses to view a foreign country, for the "spruce, capoted, brisk, sun-burnt, chattering Creoles of La Prairie afford a striking variety, and remind

---

[374] Mr. Flint might seem to imply here that he had been in Mexico. But there is no time when such a visit could easily have been made and no direct reference to it. This implication and others like it are probably the result of his realistic way of putting things.

him," that he has reached such a country. In Quebec he is struck with the great numbers of American travelers from every part of the land, and accounts for their presence there by the new facilities in traveling which have, in some sense annihilated space and time.[375]

Of travel in this country he says: "No where—give the English their due—are there finer or better found steam-boats, than those that ply between Quebec and Montreal." He had no space in which to dwell upon many things that interested him in this new land, such as the "grand spectacle of the Montmorency . . . the majestic Ottawa . . . those prodigious works of art, the Rideau and Welland Canals . . . the unique scenery about Quebec—nothing of the strange Upper Town, perched upon its eagle eyrie of rocks—nothing of the historic plains of Abraham." But he takes time to give a vivid picture of the life on one of the St. Lawrence boats, and to marvel at the beauty of nature and art on the great river's banks, where "the bleak and inexorable winter breeze but a few days since whistled over this same scenery, then a surface of snow, six feet in depth, and that this broad stream . . . was then bridged with ice, as thick and firm as the solid earth, in the midst of a desolate nature, where Winter and Death held undisputed empire."[376]

In another article, Mr. Flint tells of an interesting gathering of a few friends in Montreal, which must have occurred at this time. The conversation drifted into a discussion of books of travel. The caricatures

---

[375] *Knickerbocker*, vol. v, 244.   [376] — *Idem*, 244, 245.

in *John Bull in America* were highly appreciated by the company; but misrepresentations of Captain Hall, Major Hamilton, and Mrs. Trollope were resented by all present. One of the company present, who is represented by Mr. Flint as a "Mr. M——", but whose writings sound very much like our well known "T. F." offered to bring to the company by the next evening "a synopsis of the books of the pedantic and arrogant Captain Hall, that of the coarse flippant and vulgar man-in-petticoats, Mrs. Trollope, as well as of the impudent coxcomb, Major Hamilton." This "synopsis" is given us in nine or ten pages of an article in the *Knickerbocker* on "English Caricatures." It is not the least interesting but it is among the least admirable of Mr. Flint's literary productions which have been preserved.[377]

The northern journey, Mr. Flint says, had for him, "remembrances of recovered health, corroding anxieties laid asleep, pleasant acquaintances, and half-forgotten dreams, as gay and agreeable to dwell upon in the retrospect, as I ever expect to have of any days still reserved for me in the future of this life."[378] How long this visit was continued or just where Mr. Flint traveled after his restoration to health we do not definitely know. It is one of the places where material is short and where we would most like to know what came next in the experiences of our friend.

It is from the middle of this summer of 1834, until the seventh of November that we must place the European journey if we are to conclude that Mr. Flint made one. After the Canadian travels he would have

[377] *Knickerbocker*, vol. v, 396-408.   [378] — *Idem*, 245.

several months in which to make this trip to the old world — the world of which he had read and dreamed so much. His restored health, his leisure, easy access to the great lines of ocean travel, would suggest and make possible the trip at this time. From the reference to it [379] in May, 1835, there is no time for it later, and I do not see where there is any time for it in the years before his final location in Alexandria. If it had been earlier it hardly seems possible that such an experience would go without mention in the numerous writings which cover, almost if not quite, every year of his life up to this time.

The reference to the European experiences is as follows:

For myself, I have seen Europe, the West Indies, and South America, and have compared my impressions of what I there saw, with what I have seen in the United States and Canada. Generally speaking, we have little to compare with Europe, in point of architecture, sumptuous erections, and monuments of the arts. But, contrary to the general impression, and the arrogant boast of the European travelers among us, Boston, New-York, and Philadelphia — particularly the latter — are intrinsically handsomer towns, and strike the eye of an impartial observer, I dare be bound to say, more agreeably than most of the European capitals, in every point of view, except extent; and two of our cities sustain no mean competition with most of them, except London and Paris, even in that point of view. But our natural scenery, in many respects, incomparably exceeds that of Europe. It is out of the question that there is nothing in the old world to compare with the grandeur of our rivers, lakes, water-falls, and forests. . . The Alps and Apennines, it is true, present more elevated peaks, more sublime ranges of rock and glacier. But after all, it is naked sublimity alone, for their mountain scenery is bald, ragged, revolting. [Mr. Flint never visited the Rocky

379 *Knickerbocker*, vol. v, 397.

Mountains and seems here to have forgotten of their existence.]
Trees, verdure, cultivation, are never seen upon their higher
summits.[380]

There are several reasons for doubting whether Mr.
Flint actually visited Europe. "English Caricatures," the article in which he refers to the matter,
does not, as is usual, have his initials appended. It is
announced as "By the Author of 'Macoupin, or the
Talking Potato.'" The article is more impersonal
than is usual with Mr. Flint. It is, however, credited
to him in the index of the magazine. "Macoupin" is
also credited to him in the same way and has his initials at the end of the article. Again, if Mr. Flint
was in Europe in the summer and fall of 1834 it seems
very strange that in the extensive articles for the
Athenæum, which it would seem must have been prepared just after this time, there is no reference whatever to this experience, though there are many passages
where it might fittingly have been referred to. Dr.
James Flint does not mention it, and, what is still more
important, perhaps, is the fact that the family of Mr.
Flint, or those of them now living in Alexandria,
Louisiana, think that he never made such a journey.[381]

About the same arguments may be made against the
statement that Mr. Flint here makes in reference to
South America. There is, however, more circum-
stantial evidence for thinking that he may have been in
that part of the world. There was time for it when
he made the trip south in January, 1832. It was at
that time that he wrote his first South American story

---

[380] *Knickerbocker*, vol. v, 397.
[381] Letter of Fredric Seip, Alexandria, La., Jan. 20, 1910, in Harvard
University Library.

and that he says he gathered the material for it.[382] After this he wrote several stories which had their setting in South America. It might also have occurred at the time of the Cuban trip which is now to be mentioned, though it is hard to account for his silence about such an important part of a journey if it occurred at that time.

Mr. Flint says of the traveler:

> The requisite qualifications are, natural endowments, much previous instruction, capability of keen perception and enjoyment of the beautiful and sublime in natural scenery, a generous and philosophic mind to observe men, manners, institutions, laws, literature . . . a sincere desire to separate the true from the seeming, and more than all, an indulgent and impartial spirit, and a disposition to find enjoyment, wherever propriety and innocence allow.[383]

When he wrote these words he was moralizing over the writings of different types of travelers. However, it is a good description of Mr. Flint, the accomplished traveler, as he begins the journey of 1834-1835 and the last one of which we have any detailed account.

From New Orleans to Havana was a three to five days' journey. He did not stop in that busy mart but decided to

> Mount the *volanté*, and through lanes bounded with coffee plantations on the one hand, and cane on the other, to seek shelter among the palms.
>
> Here had I passed my winter in air, in sun, or shade, as temperature or my feelings inclined me. . . I had resided in a planter's family, in the middle condition, of which half were New-Englanders, half Creoles, catholics, easy in circumstances,

---

[382] See page 200.

[383] *Knickerbocker*, vol. v, 396. Mr. Flint's comment on the social and political importance of travel is interesting. See *Knickerbocker*, vol. iv, 168, 169.

gentle and affectionate in their intercourse, kind and forbearing to their servants, attentive to me, and their language and movements invested with an amusing, languid, sleepy kind of drawl, which I traced to their indolence and delicious climate. . . Not that the gentleman and ladies had not a full touch of human nature in their constitution here, as elsewhere.

There too was there smirking, coquetry, the infliction of bright eyes, the love of woman for new styles, the rich and poor, as in other parts of the world.[384]

Toward the middle of March he started north because "coolness fled, even from the whispering palm groves." He returned to Havana and began anew the attempt to "beguile ill health in the revolutions of perpetual change." While the negroes chattered, "and numerous casks were draying and rolling along the streets, and the dews dripped from the graceful palms, just as they will do at the same hour next March," he entered "the good ship Union for Boston." The first two days they were becalmed. Then came a storm. As usual the passengers interested Mr. Flint, and several of them are pictured for us. There were merchants, "portly, clever personages, who loved champagne, and cent per cent." They were as much out of his line as he was out of theirs. There were two passengers, however, one of whom would put herself in line with Mr. Flint and the other that he instinctively felt himself to be in line with.[385]

The first was a rich and not uncomely widow, who had just laid aside her sables for the loss of her husband who had left her, after only a few hours sickness, with a half million dollars and a son and daughter.

---

[384] *Knickerbocker*, vol. v, 279.   [385] — *Idem*, 279, 280.

Mr. Flint says of this lady: "My vanity furnishes me with no clue to explain why this lady honored me with a particular share of attention." Not only the lady but her two children, it would seem, showed the benevolent looking old gentleman "a particular share of attention." Mr. Flint was fond of children and they of him, but these two, as well as their mother seem to have been considerable of a trial to him. He was even moved to envy the departed husband and father and to conclude that there were worse evils than cholera, and that the exit of her poor husband might have been to him a merciful release.

Mr. Flint continues about this woman and her children:

Unused to slaves, this lady had estimated them more entirely the passive instruments of the caprice and tyranny of their master's family, than persons who had been born and reared amidst the indulgences of slavery. The consequence was, that these two children . . . were precisely the most annoying and mismanaged cubs, that ever sinner was tormented withal. . . They were ugly urchins, which rendered their evil manners so much the more unendurable. But what capped the climax of misery of being greased with turkey bones, and daubed with eggs, and having my books covered with ink, and my laboriously-collected herbarium scattered leaf by leaf into the sea, was, that the learned Theban of a mother was a harranguer, a tedious *preacheuse*, upon the subject of education. She had read a whole library of the modern dull books upon this theme. Most profoundly was she imbued with the theory of education; and I was placed in a dilemma of bores, between the preaching of the mother, and the practice of the children. I soon gave the imps to understand, in all practicable ways, that I was neither their step-father nor their slave. If pins sometimes happened to point upwards through my dress, when my persecutors bounced into my lap, or if they sometimes tumbled over my legs, when racing past me in the dark, I hope the charitable-minded will attribute it to accident, though I fear their mother did not.[386]

When the storm broke upon them, the third day of their voyage, Mr. Flint escaped still further from his young scourges and their lecturing mother by means of the sea-sickness which overtook them and him alike. His own sickness was not severe and it was then that he made the acquaintance of the other passenger who interested him.   He does not give her name but says that she belonged to one of the first and wealthiest families in Boston, as he afterwards learned.   She had been in Cuba for her health and was returning home in strength.   He admired her courage during the storm and discovered that it came from a reasonable view of the situation and from a well balanced mind and faith.[387]

After a sixteen days' voyage they were in Boston harbor, viewing the city of "money and hills."   Mr. Flint took leave of his young friend by telling her that when the platonic year came round, after thirty thousand calendar years had passed, he desired to be considered her declared suitor.

Mr. Flint went to the Tremont House, spending only a few days in Boston, during which time he called upon a few old time friends and made arrangements for the continuing of his travels.   While he says he

[386] *Knickerbocker*, vol. v, 280.   There is a perplexing remark made by Mr. Flint in telling the story of his experiences with this widow.   He seems to say that he himself is a widower.   Numerous references in the family letters as late as 1839, the statements made by Dr. James Flint at the time of Flint's death and the very clear and positive statements of the family, make certain that Mrs. Flint did not die until a few weeks before her husband.   The passage here referred to must be taken as a rather awkward reference to his long absence from home and to his traveling alone.

[387] *Knickerbocker*, vol. v, 281, 282.

had no purpose there "to observe, figure, or seek pleasure," yet he took occasion to call upon his young friend of the good ship Union.   He was most kindly and hospitably received – as an elder brother might be by a younger sister.   A party of the family friends were invited in to meet him.   He was introduced by the young lady to her friends, "as the person who was to stand first on the list of her declared lovers, when she should re-visit Boston, after thirty thousand years," and she declared to him that his chances should be predicated on changing nothing but the state of his health.   It was also arranged that Mr. Flint should meet some of these friends at Buffalo or Niagara Falls later in the summer.[388]

---

[388] This brief narrative of the Cuban visit and the subsequent voyage to Boston appears in the April number of the *Knickerbocker* for 1835, as "Sketches of Travel, Number Two."   The journey could not have ended until about the end of March.   The article itself must have been written in Boston about April 1.   That it appears in the April number of the magazine may be accounted for by the habits of that journal of appearing late. See *Knickerbocker*, vol. vi, 580, note.

XV. LOUISIANA AND THE LAST DAYS

Dr. James Flint says of Mr. Flint's removal to his earlier home in the south:

> In 1834, he went to the "South" to remain with his family in Alexandria, where his eldest son and daughter resided; the daughter having recently married an eminent advocate and planter of that place. He there passed the concluding years of his life in the enjoyment of competence and leisure, usually, however, spending his summers in New England, and wrote nothing excepting a *Second part of Recollections of the Mississippi Valley*, the manuscript of which he brought with him on his last visit to friends at Salem, Massachusetts, where he died, August 16th, 1840.[389]

Very little is known of the course of Mr. Flint's life during the last four or five of his three score years. Such as we have is gathered from a few letters of his family and friends. These do not furnish a continuous story.

There was not much literary work performed in this period. Besides the manuscript for the second part of the *Recollections* Doctor Flint mentions also that his cousin left revised copies of all of his principal works. Doctor Flint thought it a great desideratum that all the works should be published in a uniform edition, and improved with the revisions which his friend had left.[390] There was still another work of

[389] *Encyclopedia Americana: Supplementary Volume.*
[390] — *Idem.*

considerable extent, performed probably in the fall and winter of 1834. This was the series of eleven articles on "Sketches of the Literature of the United States," prepared for the London *Athenæum*. Much of the material is taken from earlier works but there is some new matter and it is all rearranged.

Peabody and Company of the *Knickerbocker* had suggested Mr. Flint to the London people as a suitable man for the undertaking, but a misunderstanding had arisen about the matter. Peabody and Company had asked for some money in advance in order to aid the proposed work. The money had been sent but the manuscript was not furnished either by Mr. Flint or Peabody and Company. The editors of the London magazine were not at all inclined to blame Mr. Flint, but when they learned that he had gone to Louisiana and not furnished the promised papers, for which they had advanced money, they justly felt that they had been victimized by some one. After this failure they engaged Nathaniel Parker Willis for the work.

Unexplained, this incident looks discreditable to Mr. Flint. Even so careful a student as Professor Henry A. Beers, in his *Nathaniel Parker Willis*[391] passes the matter with only the remark that Mr. Flint failed to come to time with the articles he had agreed to furnish to the *Athenæum*. In the *Athenæum*, 1835,[392] there is a letter of Mr. Flint dated at Alexandria, November 17, 1834, written to Clark and Edson, successors of Peabody and Company.

I have just received a letter directed to Peabody and Co.,

---

[391] Pages 216, 217.　　　　[392] No. 380, 105.

late of the *Knickerbocker*, from Mr. —— of the London *Athenæum*, saying that he had forwarded an order in my favor for
£20, in pay for an article on American Literature, which he understood me to have contracted to forward to that Periodical.   A
year ago, Mr. Peabody said something to me about furnishing
such an article, and I expressed my willingness to do it, after
which I heard nothing on the subject until I recently saw my
name set down in the papers, as one who was to write such an
article.   I need say no more than this to Mr. ——, to acquit
myself of the imputation, of having received pay without per-
forming the stipulated services.   If he knew me, I need not say
even this.   No order has come to my hand, nor did I stipulate
to furnish manuscript any further than as above stated.   Have
the kindness to write to him immediately, for I would not be
willing to remain a moment under the suspicion of being capable
of such a want of integrity, as would be implied in receiving
compensation, and failing to return *quid pro quo*.

This matter is best explained perhaps by the business failure of Peabody and Company sometime in
1834, and by their afterwards returning at least a part
of the £20 to the London firm.[393]   Mr. Flint's series
of articles began to appear in the July fourth number
of the *Athenæum*, 1835, and were concluded November ninth, of that year.

Mr. Flint must have felt when he returned to the
south in 1834, that his work was almost done.   His
extensive travels after this time were not on account
of business, but, as before mentioned, were for the sake
of health.   He was, it is true, only fifty-five years of
age.   But most of these years had been marked by
sickness, and many of them by severe labor and unusual exposure.   In appearance and strength he was old

---

[393] *Athenæum*, no. 375, 12, note; no. 380, 105.

beyond his years.   In 1828, at the New Year season,
he had written:

> Fondly I thought, that, years ere this, my breast
> Would cease to swell with joy or sorrow.[394]

Mr. Flint did not perform any of the duties of his
early profession in his last years.   His son James,
writing him from Harvard, addressed him as "Timothy Flint, Esq."   Other correspondents still used the
title "Reverend."   Mr. Flint sometimes seemed to
feel himself shut off from the great world in which he
had lived so actively.   There is a fragment of a letter preserved in the Boston Public Library, probably
written to Reverend Charles Lowell, and during these
last years, which shows the loneliness of the man and
his desire to keep in touch with early and far distant
friends.   He says:

> Thus I have poured out a feminine flood of gossip.   Let me
> tempt you to sin in the same way.   As I draw myself into my
> shell, abandoned by all others, let me not be forsaken by you.
> Give me your history in terms as garrulous as mine.   Let the
> record of our kindness run on till death.   You know those that
> I do and ought to remember, and will convey to them my affec-
> tionate salutation.   God bless you and yours.   T. FLINT.

His children were all with him.   Emeline, his eldest daughter, had married General Thomas in 1833.
She was a very accomplished woman, strong minded,
but not imaginative like others of the family.   For
several years before her marriage she was her father's
literary companion.   She had aided him in his extensive translations from the French, such as the *Biographie Universelle Classique.*   He speaks several
times of his co-worker.   She was also, as Mr. Flint

---

[394] *Western Monthly Review*, vol. i, 529.

was not, a Spanish scholar, and made some translations from this language for the *Western Monthly Review*. She was the second wife of General Thomas, who was a man of much force and prominence in his section of the country. He had extensive business interests and was an attorney. Soon after or possibly just before the death of her father and mother, Mrs. Thomas planned and built in Alexandria, what has been known for two generations as the Flint Homestead. It was used by General Banks as his headquarters when his army was in Alexandria during the Civil War. It is still owned and highly valued by the family.[395]

Micah Peabody, the eldest son, had married Frances Bullard, a niece of General Thomas, some time before the return of his family from the north. He had been prosperous as an attorney and planter, leaving an estate at the time of his death, valued at one hundred and fifty thousand dollars. Samuel Swett in the Harvard *Class Book for the Class of 1800*, says also that this large estate was inherited and carried on by Mr. Flint, the son having been unmarried. Both of these statements are inaccurate according to the family letters. Mr. Flint and his children together inherited Micah's estate, the wife and children of the latter having died before he did. This estate was heavily involved, and was being managed by Hubbard Flint, while his younger brother was a minor and studying law at Harvard, 1838-1841.[396]

Everything indicates that Mr. Flint was in com-

---

[395] Family letters and records, for the most part in possession of Mrs. Emeline Flint Seip, Alexandria, La. Mrs. Seip's letters, 1907-1910, have been placed in Boston Public Library.

[396] — *Idem.*

fortable circumstances in his last years. Mr. Gallagher remarks that his *Geography and History* was not only vastly popular, but vastly profitable as well.[397] He had a house of his own across the river near Alexandria, and opposite his son Micah's home at that place. This was probably in the pine woods that covered the hills opposite the village. The house here in which he lived is still standing. He operated a farm of about one hundred acres. Old account books in the possession of the family show his purchases of farm and family supplies. Mr. Flint had servants which his grandchildren think he owned, but they are not certain on this point.[398] Considering his earlier feelings and expressions on this subject, it would seem unlikely that he ever bought or owned a slave.

Mr. Flint also owned a cottage in the pine hills at Pineville, two or three miles from Alexandria, where he spent his summers. The location is still known to his family and to many people who make their home in the region. Trees and shrubs which he planted are today reverenced because of their association with the man whom all delight to honor. "Angel's Rest" and "Summerville" are named in the family letters as rallying places for the long hot seasons, during Mr. Flint's last years. Mr. Flint taught French to his young daughter, Martha Elizabeth, born in Cincinnati, 1828, while they dwelt in their summer Arcadia. But it was the son and not the father who was doing the fishing then. Another fragment of

[397] Cincinnati *Mirror*, vol. iii, 37.

[398] See letters of Emeline Flint Seip and Fredric Seip, and especially the latter's letter of Jan. 20, 1910.

the letter mentioned above, gives us a picture of their life in the pines:

> Yesterday was Sabbath and we passed the day in a general family muster and ride. But to-morrow alas! We move into town where I have to live. You all have had to undergo a double talkover – first when Micah came, and since on my return, nor were your hospitality, your beautiful [words missing from manuscript].

This fragment may indicate a recent trip to the north.[399]

Mr. Flint's home life had always been beautiful. This fact is remarked by several of his friends and it is one of the treasured traditions of his descendants. Mr. Swett says:

> His affection for his family was deep, strong, self-absorbing to an extent that we would not dare to give the slightest conception – were we not in possession of facts which speak louder than words. His wife's affection is betokened by the fact that his word to her, assuring her of his speedy dissolution, proved to be her death warrant.[400]

In the winter of 1836-1837 a great pleasure came to Mr. Flint through the visit of his cousin, Dr. James Flint. In Doctor Flint's volume of verses, the following are found:

> Lines written at sea on a voyage to visit and spend the winter with my earliest and best loved friend, Rev. T. Flint, on the banks of the Red River, for the recovery of my health. At Sea, on board the Saxon, Dec., 1836.

> Lo! my heart's nearest brother, more near than by blood,
> I come on the waves of the dark rolling flood,
> And I smile at the peril, nor shrink from the pain –
> To meet thee, my brother, on earth once again.

.   .   .   .   .   .

---

[399] Family letters. See also Appendix A.
[400] *The Christian Register*, vol. xix, 138.

I come with my brother once more to review,
Our sweet spring time when hope and her visions were new,
To live o'er again our best days of the past,
And communing of heaven, to prepare for the last.

Through thirty-six lines like the above, Doctor Flint expresses his hopes for pleasure and health. He is prepared, and half expects to leave his body in the soil where he supposes his friend will lay his dust, little knowing that they will lie together in their native soil and in a beautiful cemetery which he is soon to consecrate with other verses.[401]

In this same year, Mr. Flint was called upon to suffer the loss of his oldest son, September 15, 1837. Micah was but thirty-four years of age when he was carried away by one of the southern fevers. This son had been the pride and hope of his parents. When but twelve years of age he had written a poem, which, it is said, was printed by the Edinburgh *Review* and highly complimented by that magazine. His *Hunter and Other Poems* was published by the firm that issued the *Recollections* and at the same time. Criticisms of his son's book, Mr. Flint took as seriously as he did those of his own works. He had high hopes for Micah's development as a poet, and often shows this hope in his writings. The family say now, that he was much disappointed that Micah gave so much time to "negroes and cotton"—to quote Micah's own remark when he returned to his plantation from a visit to his parents in Cincinnati.[402] Mr. Flint worked many of his son's poems into his stories, especially into the *Shoshonee Valley*. They are found also

---

401 Flint, James. *Verses on Many Occasions*, 99, 100, 171.
402 *Knickerbocker*, vol. iii, 119.

in several numbers of the *Review* and also in the *Knickerbocker*. These poems received many favorable notices from the critics of the period. That such a son as this should be stricken down and at so early an age, and soon after the death of the wife and two little sons, Micah Jr. and James Jr., would be the heaviest loss that Mr. Flint ever met with in his family. Though the father did not allow himself to be honored with the title of the "sacred office," in this hour of his deepest grief, he rose up as the priest of his own house, and conducted over the body of his first born, the last sad rites of the Christian Church. Micah's body was buried in what is now known as the old Flint graveyard across the river from Alexandria, and where now rests the dust of most of Mr. Flint's children and grandchildren, and that of his beloved wife. Here together they await the general resurrection in the last day, when again the family circle may be complete, though one grave is in distant Salem, another in Galveston, Texas, and one, a little one, upon the shifting banks of the Great River.[403]

Micah's plantation was at Cheneyville, twenty-five or thirty miles from Alexandria. He called this place "Lunenburg," a name which it still bears. His home is yet standing at this place, and many of his former slaves proudly bear his name. He had a home also in Alexandria. His sister, Emeline Thomas, wrote of his death:

It was singularly magnanimous and calm. I have witnessed the departure of no one who seemed to have so entirely triumphed

---

[403] Family letters and records. See the Seip Letters, Boston Public Library.

over the fear of death. Until a few minutes before his last
breath, he occupied himself in sending messages to his friends.[404]

In 1839 we have another glimpse of Mr. Flint and
his family in the woods. We are glad to know that
they "are well." Early in the spring of 1839, he
made a visit to New England and returned before the
first of July.[405] Throughout his southern residence,
it was the sultry weather of March that caused Mr.
Flint the most trouble. It was this period that he
aimed to spend at the north. How often he made this
long journey during his last six years we do not know,
but it must have been several times. He knew how to
travel comfortably. He thought the time would soon
come when families would make the trip from the
south to the north and back in season, enjoying and
employing themselves in a domestic and social way
on the steam and canal boats, much as they might do
at home. He, himself, could be at home in almost any
surroundings. He could isolate himself for thought
or work when and where he would. He is said to
have translated the *Biographie Universelle* in a room
where others were talking and working.[406]

While on his northern trip in 1839, Mr. Flint
caught a severe cold, and was ill some time after his
return home. On this visit at the north he had the
added pleasure of seeing his son James Timothy at
Cambridge and also the daughter of General Thomas
who was at school in that section. James went home
in 1839, taking with him, doubtless, as he was bidden
in the home letters, "a sewing basket and water colors
for little sister Martha."

---

[404] Family letters and records.   [406] *Encyclopedia Brittanica.*
[405] — *Idem.*

Early in May of 1840, James was still at home, and accompanied his father on the steamer to Natchez, as he started for the north.   It was much later than Mr. Flint was in the habit of making this trip.   It does not seem that he was compelled to go on account of his health, though he was not well.   He had it in mind, of course, to make a visit, and perhaps chiefly, to arrange for the publication of the second part of the *Recollections* which he had with him.   The revision of his other works was also completed [407] and he doubt-less hoped to arrange for their publication.

At Natchez they were waiting for a steamer which should take Mr. Flint up the river, when they were overtaken by a tornado.   Mr. Venable says of this storm:

> At one o'clock of the sultry afternoon of Thursday, May 7, a furious storm sweeps along the river, whirls the shipping to destruction, tears the city.   "Never, never, never was there such desolation and ruin," was the word of the Natchez *Courier* next day.   The loss of property was immense, and not fewer than four hundred people were killed. . . The Natchez *Free Trader* mentioned that among those who were taken out alive, were "Timothy Flint, the historian and geographer, and his son from Natchitoches, Louisiana." [408]

In one of the last letters that he ever wrote, Mr. Flint tells of this experience.   The letter was written from North Reading, and probably to his classmate, Samuel Swett.   At any rate, the latter included it in the article on the death of his friend in the *Christian Register*.   Only a part of the letter was used and it is as follows:

[407] *Encyclopedia Americana: Supplementary Volume.*

[408] Venable, William H.   *Beginnings of Literary Culture in the Ohio Valley*, 360.

The morning preceding the storm had been excessively sultry. The sky was overcast rather, as it appeared, with a sort of dusty haze than thick clouds — and the sky from nine to one was a continual rumble of a hundred low thunders all melting into each other, and no rain fell. At half after one, there sat at the hotel table, I suppose, fifty guests. The thunder had within a few minutes become severe, and the darkness so great as to require candles. But these circumstances are not apt in that climate to create alarm. I finished a hasty dinner and went through a reading room, and a beautiful bar-room to the front door looking up the street, for it was Natchez under the hill. I saw a terrific looking black cloud, as though a well defined belt of black broad cloth, seeming a mile and a half wide, shooting up the river bluff with fearful velocity. At the end it poured out dark wreaths, resembling those of the steam-boat pipe. I ran to the reading room for James, bidding him take my arm and follow me into the street. But as we made for the front door, the windows and doors blew in. The boats were seen dashing into the river, and the air was black and full of flying fragments. There was a general rush for the front door. The rush closed the passage, and kickings, fighting, and cursing ensued. Part were trampled under foot, and part, such as James and I, thrown over their heads. They, fortunately for us, threw us and three more into a place, where we were destined to be saved. It was between the bar room and the reading room. I felt the pillars reel, seized one of them, and expected the next moment to have all my maladies effectually cured. The next moment every thing came down with a crash like the blow of a hammer, and the whole pile chimneys and all were packed as closely as if they had been taken down and piled. Water poured upon us like a torrent, and we were as dark as Egypt. James had been separated from me. I found myself alive though much bruised and crushed, and a nail had gone through my hat and grazed my temple, so as to cause some bleeding. My first word was for "James! James! are you alive?" The answer was, "I am. Are you living, Father?" We were saved by the arching of two or three beams, that resisted all that came upon them. He crawled through the mud and got hold of my hand. The timbers gave us four inches. After being there, perhaps, half an hour, we were extricated. The town under the hill, boats and all, were a wreck – in fact, the latter all sunk and gone. Many bodies were dug from our house, and the whole spectacle was one of sickening horror. I was many hours covered with mud, and under a drenching rain, before I could recover any clothes or get a shelter. The crown of James's hat was cut from his head, just grazing the top of the skull. He returned home, after seeing me on an upcountry boat. The season had been the warmest ever known, and we had had two months of high summer. The weather turned very cold, the night I began to ascend the river, and my long drenching and exposure, with my previous sickness, gave me severe chills. They followed me all the way here, and contributed, I have no doubt, to my present condition.

I had not thought when I began, that I could scrawl so much. Take it, not for what it is worth, but for what it has cost me. You will, probably, be one of my last correspondents. At any rate, I can only loose the memory of your kindness to me and mine with life. I am, dear sir, gratefully and affectionately yours,   TIMOTHY FLINT.[409]

This letter was written from the home of his brother, Peter Flint. It was not at the house of their birth but a mile or so to the west of the village of North Reading, and near the place where the remains of their father and mother were probably buried. In this home was a little granddaughter whose duty and privilege it was to comb and brush the silver hair of her great uncle, and who thirty-four years later, when writing a letter to the almost unknown cousins in the south, was proud to tell them how she cherished the memory of Reverend Timothy Flint, and this childhood ministry to the dying man.[410]

[409] *The Christian Register*, vol. xix, 138, 139.

[410] Letter of C. A. Clark, North Reading, Mass., July 26, 1874, in possession of Mrs. Seip.

lot which was used for the first time when the friend and father was buried in it.[414]   Fifteen years later it received the body of Dr. James Flint, which rests just beside that of his "more than brother."   Several members of Doctor Flint's family are buried here also, but the circle was not completed until about a year ago, when the last child of Doctor Flint, Miss Amelia G. Flint, ninety-two years of age, was buried there. The graves of the two friends occupy the center of the lot.   "David and Jonathan" are united in death as they were in life.

Over the grave of Mr. Flint was erected a simple monument, eight or nine feet in height, with the following inscription written by Doctor Flint.[415]

REV. TIMOTHY FLINT

Whose writings have won for him deserved
celebrity, was born in Reading, Mass., 1780,
where he died on a visit from the South,
August 16, 1840, aged 60.

He painted on his glowing page,
    The peerless valley of the West;
That shall in every coming age,
    His genius and his toils attest.

---

[414] Harmony Grove Cemetery *Records* (Salem). Both Dr. James Flint and Timothy Flint were much interested in the beautifying of burial places. The latter once visited Mount Auburn Cemetery, Boston, and greatly enjoyed its beauty and care. As he wandered over it with a friend, some of its hillside views made him imagine the pines saying:
    "Oh, lay me in the spot where the sunbeams rest,
    When they promise a glorious morrow;"
                                    — *Knickerbocker*, vol. ii, 257, 258.

[415] An exact copy of this inscription is preserved in Doctor Flint's *Verses on Many Occasions*. Also in a manuscript copy in Boston Public Library which had been sent to Mrs. Coffin by Doctor Flint in 1841, just as it had been "prepared by his bereaved and still loving kinsman and friend."

TIMOTHY FLINT'S MONUMENT, HARMONY GROVE
CEMETERY, SALEM, MASSACHUSETTS

But wouldst thou, gentle pilgrim, know
　　What worth, what love endeared the man?
This the lone hearts that miss him, show
　　Better than storied marble can.

XVI. LITERARY TRAITS AND ESTIMATES

Mr. Flint did not expect to win an enduring fame by means of his writings. He knew too well the fate of the many masterful minds and true geniuses, of his own and other days, to hope that he would escape the almost universal doom of being soon forgotten. On this point he moralizes when he is reviewing the novels of Charles Brockden Brown.[416] Mr. Flint felt himself in close sympathy with Mr. Brown at many points. They were alike "blighted by the mildews of disease almost from birth." Mr. Brown, too, was compelled to write for his daily bread, incessantly until his fragile frame was worn out. He had reached what Flint held as his ideal: deep feeling, powerful moral painting, laying open the recesses of the heart.

While Timothy Flint did not think he would be remembered as a litterateur, he thought he was preserving matters of interest for the future historian. In the advertisement to the *Western Monthly Review*,[417] he says:

> We can easily enjoy in anticipation, the eagerness, with which the future historian will repair to them, as a synopsis, of most of what has been said, and written, in the Western Country, touching its own natural, moral, and civil history.

[416] American novelist, 1771-1810. See Flint's article in *Western Monthly Review*, vol. i, 483-494.

[417] Vol. i, p. iii.

Professor Henry A. Beers[418] says:

> That Flint had a glimmering sense of what fiction might some day accomplish as a real contribution to sociology, is indicated on page 148, volume ii, of *Arthur Clenning*: "A fair history of the society of a country village [would be a thousand times more interesting than a novel; and besides the interest of the picture, it would be one of the most useful views of society that can be presented. But taste has not yet matured sufficiently to relish such a picture, and, perhaps, the historian does not yet exist who has the requisite discrimination and felicity to draw it!]

In *George Mason* the moral purpose is always in evidence often to the detriment of art in the story. He often stops to point out the moral, to preach and to exhort. The "genuine American" motto, "Don't give up the ship," is often brought in though it must be dragged in bodily. It is in this book that he says:

> I write for the young, the poor, and the desolate; and the moral maxim which I wish to inculcate is, that we ought never to despond either in our religious or our temporal trials.

In this work he is concerned with "the short and simple annals of the poor" because nine in ten of the human race are of that class.[419]

But Mr. Flint is not always or only utilitarian in his writings. He values literature for its civilizing and ennobling powers. It is worthy of culture simply as an art. One of his chief regrets expressed in a number of articles on the subject and notably in the series published in the *Athenæum*,[420] is, that literature is in such a low state in the country. He re-

---

[418] Letter of Henry A. Beers, Dec. 12, 1907, in Library of Harvard University.

[419] Flint, Timothy. *George Mason*, 3, 4.

[420] Volume for 1835.

grets that people are so absorbed in business and politics, that there is almost no time left for encouraging the high and necessary art of the literary worker. He lamented the lack of taste in the reading public, and all that tends to degrade it among publishers and reviewers. He thought one of the greatest weaknesses of the American literary world was that it had not cut loose from its English models and bid defiance to the pride and conceit of the English world of letters. At this point he shows, as on many other occasions, his dislike of things English. He would turn from England to the continent for ideals and inspiration. For himself, he goes to the French but he sees that Germany is to be, and already is, the leader in the search for truth and in cosmopolitan scholarship.[421] He was much interested in, and hopeful concerning, the beginning that was being made by a little group of Harvard men to introduce the German thought and literature into the United States. It promised well for a new and worthy school in America.

Mr. Griswold says:

> Flint was compelled to write constantly and rapidly, and to print without revision.[422]

This may well be true. His letters are as accurate as his printed page. And lack of finish is one of the greatest evils of the page, and the story as well. There are so many obvious faults, in plot, sentences, and even in use of words, that one often regrets that he did not spend more time in the revising of his work. At such times new regrets arise, that the revised copies of his

---

[421] *Western Monthly Review*, vol. iii, 267, 278.
[422] Griswold, Rufus W. *Prose Writers of America*, 153.

principal works which Doctor Flint mentions,[423] are not thus far discovered.

Of one common fault, Mr. Flint pleads that he is not guilty in any way that it is possible to avoid, that of deliberately emptying other people's books into his own. No one is disposed to charge him with this fault. He was quite free, however, to pour his own books into each other. This is notably true in the *Geography and History* as depending on long passages from the *Recollections*. The *Indian Wars* is little more than a compilation from the *Geography and History*. Many paragraphs and pages in succession are carried over without other changes than those made by the printer. This is not true in the case of *Daniel Boone*. The same scenes and incidents which occur in the earlier work are here entirely rewritten. In his stories he often takes a page or two of description, or an incident, from the inexhaustible *Geography and History,* and this work supplies material also for the *Review*. He makes a generous use of his son Micah's poetry in his stories, notably in the *Shoshonee Valley*. There is in this story a curious adaptation of one of Micah's poems. "Frederick" standing on the Chinese shore and gazing out into the sea where a few leagues away the beloved "Jessy" had disappeared into the depths, recites a few lines that have a familiar sound for they recall the lines of Micah P. Flint. In truth three verses of Micah's "Lines, on Passing the Grave of my Sister" have been adapted by the father and put into Frederick's mouth.[424]

---

[423] *Encyclopedia Americana: Supplementary Volume.*

[424] Flint, Timothy. *Shoshonee Valley*, vol. ii, 262; *Western Monthly Review*, vol. i, 652, 653.

Dullness never appeared to Mr. Flint as dignity. He chose always the language of the heart. To be prosy or dull seemed to him almost a sin to be ranked with dishonesty. The *Britannica* says: "His style was vivid, plain, forcible, and his matter always interesting." Of his style in writing and speaking Mr. Flint says upon one occasion, "We admit ourselves, that we have a pernicious attachment to ornamented speech." [425]

Professor Henry A. Beers, when writing his life of Nathaniel Parker Willis, about 1885,[426] had occasion to examine Mr. Flint's articles on "Sketches of the Literature of the United States," in the *Athenæum* in 1835, as they were related to similar articles of Mr. Willis published in the same volume of the *Athenæum*. About Mr. Flint's articles, Professor Beers remarks that they amply made up in heaviness any want of ballast in Willis. He thought them full of general views which if not correct, were harmless because unreadable. Professor Beers says of *Arthur Clenning*, however, that it is by no means without merit:

> It has imagination and enough imaginative art to secure interest. Ecce Signum – I have read it through, and so have two other members of my family – a feat not always possible in the case of a modern novel of much greater pretensions.[427]

This feat is the more striking when it is known that it was accomplished in two days' time, and the story has about the same number of words as the average modern novel.

Mr. Venable thinks there was never a more delight-

[425] *Western Monthly Review*, vol. i, 749.
[426] Beers, Henry A. *Nathaniel Parker Willis*, 217.
[427] Letter, Dec. 12, 1907.

ful book of the kind written than the *Recollections*.
He says:

A more original book it would be impossible to conceive of.
In fact, it seems not to be a book, but a familiar talk – a picture
from nature; a man revealing himself to the sympathetic world
with unconscious and complete candor, confidence and enthusiasm.[428]

He thinks the novels, especially *Francis Berrian*,
racy and readable to this day.

Mr. Gallagher thought this first novel of Mr.
Flint worth, for its descriptions alone, a score of the
English novels that were being reprinted every day in
this country. The fact that Mr. Gallagher wrote
about Mr. Flint and his work while Mr. Flint still
lived in Cincinnati, and the considerable measure of
success that he himself had in the literary field, make
his remarks and estimates of unusual value. Although he was an ardent admirer of Mr. Flint and
had read his *Recollections*, the *Geography and History* and *Francis Berrian* again and again, and hoped
to read them yet more, and while he read he had no
thought of time, he was not blind to the faults. He
was free also to speak of them.[429] He thought his
friend's style was in defiance of the schools, obnoxious
to criticism, but of great force and often much beauty.
He says:

Disdaining the trammels which the masters would impose on
him, he soars into the regions of poetry. Consequently he for-
gets not infrequently, that there is such a thing in composition
as ending a sentence.

This highly poetic style, Mr. Gallagher thought,

---

428 Venable, William H., *Beginnings of Literary Culture in the Ohio
Valley*, 358.

429 Cincinnati *Mirror*, vol. iii, 36, 37.

was hardly suitable for scientific works. He had himself found it a great annoyance. It was too interesting to be useful. In looking for facts in the pages of the *Geography and History* one forgot his quest or having found the facts he forgot himself and went on and on in the thrilling narrative. Mr. Gallagher did not know of Flint's equal in the English language, in descriptive writing. Of this power he says, he would feast his eye upon some scene of beauty, to him of surpassing loveliness, seize his pen – the divine afflatus upon him – and page after page would soon be glowing with the eloquence and fervency of his nature.[430]

Mr. Gallagher thought carelessness and voluminous writing was Mr. Flint's greatest weakness. In the latter part of the Cincinnati period, when Mr. Gallagher was writing of him as the first man in the western group of writers –"a group only ten years behind the Atlantic circles"– Mr. Flint was very productive and seemed to his friend, not to be adding to his fame. "Capability," Mr. Gallagher thought, was the one word that summed up and described Mr. Flint's mental traits. He says:

> Besides John Neal, there is no one who can produce in a certain time, so many volumes on so many subjects, and generally so well executed, as Timothy Flint.[431]

Mr. Flint's style both accounts for his interest in French literature, and is itself accounted for by the influence of that literature. His interest in French writers was so strong toward the close of his literary career, that he did little more than translate and comment upon the works of the men that most interested him. This was not a late interest, however, for he

---

[430] Cincinnati *Mirror*, vol. iii, 36.   [431] — *Idem.*

tells that in college he was a student of French writers. There is no doubt that one of the reasons for the failure of his magazine was that he lived too much in European, and especially in French literature and history. In this, as in his missionary work, and his religious views, he was in advance of his age so far that they left him alone or only threw stones after him. His translations from the *Genie du Christianisme* had been "cradled" in many papers but not credited to him.[432]

Perhaps the most extensive work that Mr. Flint ever undertook was that upon which he was engaged in the early part of 1830, the translation of the *Dictionaire Historique, ou Biographie Universelle Classique*. Upon the basis of this and the work of Lempriere, he proposed to construct an *American Biographical Dictionary*. Upon the translation he had his oldest daughter's help. In April, 1830, he had made a good beginning of six hundred manuscript pages and had gotten well along with the b's. In June he had gotten on to "D'JENGUYS." The translations were probably finished, but whether the *American Biographical Dictionary* was completed there are no means of knowing. The closing article in the last number of the *Review* is a translation from the *Dictionaire Historique d'Education*, which he had been admiring a few months earlier and wishing some competent translator would undertake to put into English.[433]

Some of the estimates that were made of Mr. Flint's

---

432 *Western Monthly Review*, vol. iii, 534.
433 — *Idem*, vol. iii, 534, 582, 663, also 587, 666.

literary work by his contemporaries may be further noted. N. P. Willis, in his *American Monthly Magazine*[434] for 1829, spoke strongly of the value of Mr. Flint's magazine and historical work as contributions to the knowledge of the west, and mentioned the *Shoshonee Valley* as showing the influence of the white people upon the Indians.   In the *Athenæum*[435] Mr. Willis said, that he was really a man of talent, and that *Francis Berrian* was his best work.   The New York *Observer*,[436] said that he ranked among the more distinguished writers of the country.   His classmate, Samuel Swett, said:

> Mr. Flint was one of the most distinguished of our literary characters, especially at the west.

His *Recollections*, Swett thought was to be an everlasting monument to his fame.[437]

William Cullen Bryant made a very favorable review of the first edition of the *Geography and History* in the New York *Evening Post*.   Mr. Flint says of this notice (no copy of which has been found), "If any one were not proud, he would be more or less than man."[438]

Griswold said,

> It [the *Geography and History*] was at that time the most important contribution which had been made to American geography, and, with the *Recollections*, it embraces the most graphic and faithful descriptions of the scenery and physical aspect of the western states that has ever yet been written.[439]

[434] Vol. i, 75.
[435] Vol. for 1835, no. 375, 12.
[436] Vol. xviii, 139.
[437] *Christian Register*, vol. xix, 138.
[438] Flint, Timothy. *History and Geography*, p. xiii.
[439] Griswold, *op. cit.*, 152.

Henry T. Tuckerman[440] speaks of Flint as extensively read, widely beloved, as at home in the wilderness, a favorite in society, the peculiar value of his writings being that they evince not a cursory survey of regions described but of years of residence. Besides this intimate contact with men and countries he had the power of patient observation. Tuckerman believed that Flint's books would often be consulted by subsequent writers.

The New York *Commercial* – quoted by Mr. Gallagher in his *Mirror*[441] – thinks the *Geography and History,* and the *Recollections* the most valuable contributions that industry and research have ever produced for the making known of the western interior. Mr. Flint is, this critic thinks, one of the most excellent writers that the country has produced, and belongs to that very rare class in the country, "authors or litterateurs." He says also that Mr. Flint is almost as versatile as Goldsmith, that he is distinguished as a novelist, naturalist, geologist, geographer, and essayist. His ethical productions seem to this writer to show a mind strong and cultivated, a judgment unwarped and sound, with a sense of religion of the most purifying influence. This writer's only lament is that Mr. Flint has not been more widely appreciated.

Mrs. Trollope thinks no better of America's literature than of her other characteristics, but she has a good word for Mr. Flint. She says:

Mr. Flint's *Francis Berrian* is delightful. There is a vigor and freshness in his writing that is exactly in accordance with

---

440 *America and Her Commentators. With a Critical Sketch of Travel in the United States,* 402, 404.

441 Cincinnati *Mirror,* vol. iii, 444.

what one looks for in the literature of a new country; and yet, strange to say, is exactly what is most wanting in that of America. . . His *History of the Mississippi Valley* is a work of great interest and information, and will, I hope, in time find its way to England, where I think it is much more likely to be appreciated than in America.[442]

The United States *Literary Gazette*[443] of Boston for May 15, 1826, gives a dozen pages of quotations from the *Recollections*. The reviewer makes few remarks about the work except that it is by one very competent to write and not of the common class of tourists. It is, he thinks, a very important subject upon which the older section of the country needs to be accurately and fully informed, and he quotes fully for the benefit of those who may not see the book.

The *Southern Review*[444] gives an extended review of the *Recollections*. The reviewer has carefully read the work, and gives a very accurate itinerary of Mr. Flint's journeyings, which can not be made out without careful reading and rereading. With the quotations and synopsis given in this review, we have a very good presentation of the whole work. But even then the reviewer says:

When we look back on what we are compelled to omit, we can not but feel regret. We feel sorrow at closing the volume and bidding our friend adieu, and can not refrain from sincerely wishing him a re-establishment of his health, and a long life of happiness and utility in the bosom of his amiable family.

Concerning the character of this "Presbyterian Minister from New England," this writer says:

He is, evidently, a man of sound observation, of liberal prin-

---

[442] Trollope, Mrs., *op. cit.*, vol. ii, 155.
[443] Vol. iv, 133-146.
[444] Vol. ii, 192-216.

ciples, of engaging simplicity, pure benevolence, and unaffected piety. . . Though a man of education, he does not appear to be one of science; or if so, he has carefully avoided displaying it.

This man is very much pleased with Mr. Flint's unprejudiced views on the slavery question, and with his advice to the people of the north against the political agitation and abuse of the question.

The *American Monthly Review* [445] devotes eight pages to a review of Flint's *History and Geography*. The reviewer is occupied with pointing out the errors of fact, or supposed errors, the infelicities of the language and the absurdities of certain statements. Some of these charges are true. Mr. Flint is not always clear in his statements. Some of his statements are far too general when they should have been definite. In other cases, it is probable that Mr. Flint knew of what he was speaking better than the reviewer. For instance, the reviewer states that Mr. Birkbeck had nothing to do with Mr. Flower's founding of Albion, Illinois. He seems to be ignorant of the fact that Mr. Flower and Mr. Birkbeck bought a tract of land together, divided it by lot and labored together for the building up of the settlement on the English Prairie where both Albion and Wanborough were located. [446]

The editor of the *Knickerbocker*, probably Charles Fenno Hoffman, [447] was an admirer of Flint. In March, 1833, he gives six pages of the translation of Droz's *Art of Being Happy*. He speaks of the trans-

---

[445] Vol. iv, 460-468.

[446] See Thwaites's *Early Western Travels*, vol. ix, 71, note; vol. x, 47, note, 271, 272.

[447] *Knickerbocker*, vol. ii, 110; vol. iii, 320.

lator as, our eloquent countryman.   In the same volume he reviews the *Lectures upon Natural History*. He says:

> The name of Mr. Flint begins to be well known to his countrymen as that of one of the very best of our native writers.

He approves of the aim of the book and speaks of the style as, "like all of the writings of the author, flowing, warm and animated." [448]

On the other hand is the *American Monthly Review* [449] which had to read the same *Lectures* with "our smelling bottle in hand."   It was not from fear of the cholera, nor from the bad odor arising from the book, nor yet from a proneness to fainting, but

> To prevent heart sinking, we were obliged to stimulate our nasal extremity, while we read. . .   Such continued deep plowing of our sensibilities, such delectable outpouring of waters of pathos, such wild visions of fancy, hanging round grave and solemn preaching, like mistletoe on an oak, such snuffs, mere finger pinches of philosophy, mingled with wholesale absurdities, were altogether too much for our poor, mechanical, straightforward humanity.   We trust there are natures to which this book will be like mother's milk, natural food.

It is the high sounding title of the work and its very general and popular character which seems to be most offensive to the editor of the *American Monthly Review*.   The title of the book is a mere bait, he thinks. It is not fair because it does not say that important lectures are translations.   The editor has not time to point them out but he warns the reader that the book is full of errors.   It has great honesty of purpose united with great credulity.   The credulity is that of poetry,

---

[448] *Knickerbocker*, vol. i, 140-146, and 193, 194.
[449] Vol. iii, 261.

and altogether too credulous for natural history. The reviewer says:

> Hence it is that furies with snaky hair, no longer people the regions of imagination, but under our author's hand would become every day sort of folk. He tells us that he has actually seen a hair – plucked from the living horse, and thrown into a trough of water, exposed to the genial rays of a warm sun, turn to a living snake.[450]

The editor thinks that Mr. Flint has destroyed a beautiful fable by believing it a fact.

> Still, with all his exuberance and wildness . . . Mr. Flint has made a useful book. Its object is noble. Even with all his faults, his inflated style, and all its puerilities and gross inaccuracies the book has many redeeming virtues, and for the hour is a pleasant companion.

But it is vain to look for a little appreciation of the work. The reviewer is off again upon his old way of ridicule:

> There is no system, and the author pretends to none.

You are not led softly into the realms of mystery but:

> You are seized by the collar, and pitched heels over head into the fathomless ocean of science. As you scramble ashore all dripping and covered with sea-weed, the author again grasps you and introduces you to some great picture.

---

[450] *American Monthly Review*, vol. iii, 264. This reference is to page 49 of the *Lectures* and is as follows: "I have observed an analogous fact, appertaining to another branch of natural history. I heard the fact asserted and denied, and I made the trial myself. A long black hair from a horse's mane was left in a wooden trough, to soak in rain water, during the sultry days of August, for ten or twelve days. At the end of that time it had become white, and had acquired a protuberance at one extremity, like a head. It moved about, folded and unfolded itself, showed sensibility when touched, and had become in fact that singular animal, of which naturalists, as far as I know, have taken no notice; but which farmers know well by the name hair-snake."

Again and more fairly:

> This is the great fault of the book before us; there is a want
> of impressive distinctness. . . It is truly to be lamented that
> one who knows so well how to color and embody with life such
> facts, should allow his imagination to usurp the throne of his
> judgment.

The style of this reviewer is that of the smart newspaper paragrapher and there appears to be a personal
dislike of Mr. Flint. But he has pointed out the evident weaknesses of the author. His suggestion that
Mr. Flint might honor his former profession, the
ministry, by thinking more and writing less, is of
course unkind, but it is none the less true.

The London *Quarterly Review* [451] for 1832, gives
twenty pages to a review of the *Recollections*. Most
of this is in fine print, quoting from Mr. Flint's work.
It is for the most part favorable, but the reviewer has
not read the work closely enough to follow Mr. Flint's
movements. He thinks that Mr. Flint lived longest
at Jackson, Missouri, and that he made one visit to
New England during the first ten years of his western
residence. The impression of the reviewer concerning the work as a whole is worth notice. He says:

> We wish Mr. Timothy Flint had fallen in our way before
> we drew up our account of Mrs. Trollope *On the Domestic
> Manners of the Americans*, because the two writers travel over
> much of the same ground, and the contrasts as well as the paral-
> lels, which their descriptions of nature and society present, are full
> of interest. Having lost the opportunity of presenting them
> together — we must be contented with expressing our hope that
> these *Recollections* may be reprinted in this country, and placed
> in every library of voyages and travels, on the same shelf with

[451] Vol. xlviii, 201-222.

those two little volumes which seem to have proved such bitter chewing to our Radicals and Whigs. With obvious faults, Mr. Flint's style is marked by countervailing excellencies, being lively, flowing, often vigorous, and, in general, quite unaffected; but this is a secondary merit. These pages reflect a sincere, humane, and liberal character, a warm and gentle heart and hardly even a prejudice that is not amiable.

The reviewer is in full sympathy with Mr. Flint except that he is "pulled up" by the unfavorable comparison of the present European nations with the ancient people of America known as Moundbuilders.

Of such poor bigotry, based on such solid ignorance, we should never have expected to discover a specimen in the same book with the beautiful passages we have been quoting. Here, however, is the Yankee mark.

The *North American Review* for October, 1826,[452] in reviewing the *Recollections* says:

This volume has been perused by us with great pleasure, and with much respect for the writer's talents and character. We have risen from it, indeed, with a stronger sympathy, than we should wish to have occasion to feel with the author in the hardships and sufferings endured by him and his family; with more vivid conceptions than we before possessed, of the peculiar aspects of the grand and beautiful features of the country he describes; with more enlarged views of its natural resources, of the extent and progress of its population; and with more favorable impressions of the general character of our fellow citizens of those vast and fertile regions, that border upon the Mississippi, and its mighty tributary streams from the east and the west.

.   .   .   .

Mr. Flint is not one of the common herd of travel writers and journal makers "who" as he remarks, "travel post or are wafted through a country in a steamboat, and assume, on the ground of having thus traversed it, to know all about it." [453]

---

[452] Vol. xxiii, 355-368.   [453] — *Idem*, 357.

Still more to the purpose the reviewer thinks, is the fact that Mr. Flint's

Intellectual, moral, and literary qualifications fitted him to avail himself of these advantages, and to impart attractions and an interest to his narrative, which such qualifications only can impart to a work of this kind. He unites properties which do not often meet in the same mind, a capacity for discriminating and philosophic observation, a true tact and common sense logic, with the imagination, feeling, and romantic sentiment of the poet and novelist. . . His deep and vivid sympathy with the varying aspects of the physical universe, which opened to his view in the Western world, gives to his narrative one of its most peculiar and engaging features. There is a truth, a distinctness, a graphic fidelity in his descriptions, which make the reader feel himself to be a present spectator of the objects and occurrences he describes. . . As he feels strongly and deeply, he heightens, no doubt, by the coloring of his imagination, the hues of the gay or sad vicissitudes which befell him. Yet there is an air of good faith and reality in what he relates, which convinces us, that we may listen to him with the confidence, with which a man, at his fireside, receives the communications of a friend of tried integrity, telling the tale of his eventful wanderings and various fortunes after an absence of many years.[454]. . It has the peculiar charm of an autobiography, written by a man of cultured intellect, disclosing his thoughts and the hidden workings of his soul, under various novel circumstances. . . The reflections are often original and sensible, and indicate a mind accustomed to hold "large discourse, looking before and after," and rich in its own resources.

In the closing paragraph of this review, the faults are pointed out. The reviewer does not mean to be unjust, and is not, when he says:

An obvious fault in this work is the confusion, which the reader experiences in its perusal, arising from the circumstance, that the author seems sometimes to be writing at Alexandria, some-

[454] *North American Review*, vol. xxiii, 358.

times in New England, and at other times it is difficult to con-
jecture where.   Instances of repetition in thought and language
frequently occur.   The same word is often repeated ungrace-
fully in the same sentence, where a synonym would save the
awkwardness, and express the sense equally well.   The thread-
bare quotation, "longing, lingering look behind," comes upon
us something like a half dozen times.   Many parts of the work
bear evident marks of haste in the composition.   We notice these,
not as flagrant faults, but as blemishes, which a little more attention, or careful revision would have prevented.

This review makes extensive quotations from the
work and is perhaps the best of the several that were
written.

The *North American Review* did not soon forget
Mr. Flint.   It occasionally referred to him for several
years after his retirement.   In July, 1836, it said:

Flint's *Ten Years' Residence* is one of our few genuine national works.   It could have been written nowhere but in the
Western Valley.   It could have been written by no one, whose
mind had not been moulded by a constant contact with western
scenery and people.

The reviewer was speaking of another writer's work
in lines similar to those of Mr. Flint.   This writer
seems to have criticised Flint's work as a failure.   The
Review remarks:

He will have added to his already well-earned fame, when
he shall have produced such a "failure" as Mr. Flint's *Ten Years
Residence in the Mississippi Valley.*[458]

---

[458] Vol. xliii, 2.